POETRY AND PSYCHIATRY
Essays on Early Twentieth-Century
Russian Symbolist Culture

STUDIES IN SLAVIC AND RUSSIAN LITERATURES, CULTURES, AND HISTORY

Series Editor:
Lazar FLEISHMAN (*Stanford University*)

ACADEMIC
STUDIES
PRESS

POETRY AND PSYCHIATRY

*Essays
on Early Twentieth-Century
Russian Symbolist Culture*

MAGNUS LJUNGGREN

Translated
by Charles Rougle

BOSTON / 2014

Library of Congress Cataloging-in-Publication Data:
A bibliographic record for this title is available
from the Library of Congress.

Copyright © 2014 Academic Studies Press
All rights reserved.

ISBN 978-1-61811-350-4 (cloth)
ISBN 978-1-61811-361-0 (electronic)
ISBN 978-1-61811-369-6 (paper)

Book design by Ivan Grave
On the cover: Sergey Solovyov and Andrey Bely, 1904.

Published by Academic Studies Press in 2014
28 Montfern Avenue
Brighton, MA 02135, USA
press@academicstudiespress.com
www.academicstudiespress.com

Table of Contents

List of Illustrations	6
Introduction	8
Andrey Bely and the Philosopher's Nephew	10
Bely and Aleksandr Blok	18
The Symbolist with Two Careers	26
Symbolism's Charlatan	35
Oracle or Quack?	43
Janko Lavrin—Pan-Slavist across the Spectrum	54
The "Swede" in the Late Nineteenth- and Early Twentieth-Century Russian Culture— and His Daughter	61
Blok and Strindberg's Face	68
The Early Breakthrough of Psychoanalysis in Russia	88
Anthroposophy's Decade in Russia	98
Bely's Encounter with Rudolf Steiner	107
Freud's Unknown Russian Patient	115
Emilii Medtner and Carl Gustav Jung	124
Boris Pasternak and Goethe	134
Marietta Shaginyan and Verner von Heidenstam	138
Literature	144
Index of Names	149

List of Illustrations

Sergey Solovyov, 1904	11
Sergey Solovyov and Andrey Bely in Dedovo, 1905	12
Andrey Bely, 1916	14
Lyubov and Aleksandr Blok, 1903	20
Andrey Bely, 1904	21
Aleksandr Blok, 1907	22
Lev Kobylinsky, 1897	28
Lev Polivanov	28
Leonid Pasternak's sketch of Ellis (Lev Kobylinskij), Nikolay Berdyaev and Andrey Bely attending a lecture by Vyacheslav Ivanov in 1910	31
Valentin Sventsitsky, 1910s.	38
Anna Mintslova, 1905	46
Andrey Bely, 1922	52
Janko Lavrin portrayed by Boris Kustodiev, 1909	55
The cover of Janko Lavrin's *In the Land of Eternal War*, Petrograd 1916	60
Aleksey Venkstern and his wife Olga a few years before his death	62
Double cousins Natalya Venkstern and Sofya Giatsintova, undated	63
Aleksandr Vyakhirev, undated	65
Mikhail Bulgakov as the judge in *The Pickwick Papers*, 1934	66
Vladimir Pyast a couple of years before his trip to Stockholm	69
Aleksandr Blok, 1911	70
Vladimir Pyast's message to Strindberg in a signed envelope	75
Nikolay Kulbin's portrait of Strindberg, 1912	81

Pioneers of Psychoanalysis: Osip Feltsman, Nikolay Vyrubov, and Nikolay Osipov, 1914	89
Sigmund Freud among Russians. On his left, Max Eitingon, on the right, Moisey Vulf	91
Sergey Pankeev, the Wolfman, circa 1910	92
"Little Friday" meeting at the Moscow University Psychiatric Clinic in April 1911. In the middle row on the far right Nikolay Osipov, Mikhail Asatiani, and Osip Feltsman. Third from the left in the front row, dean of Russian psychiatry Vladimir Serbsky	95
Rudolf Steiner, 1916	100
Nikolay Berdyaev, 1912	101
Andrey Bely, 1912	103
Andrey Bely, 1916	105
Bely's drawing of Nikolay Ableukhov in *Petersburg*	108
The view from Bely's hotel window in Vitznau. Photo: Martin Ryf	110
Andrey Bely and Asya Turgeneva, 1912	111
Bely's "Lifeline"—an attempt to summarize his personal and artistic evolution and important influences from his first conscious moments in 1883 at the age of 2-3 up to 1927, when he drew the sketch	114, 152-153
Ivan Ilyin, 1916	119
Vyacheslav Ivanov, 1913	121
Ivan Ilyin as *The Thinker* by Mikhail Nesterov, 1921-1922	123
Emilii Medtner on the right, with his brother Nikolay and wife Anna in Nizhny Novgorod, 1904	125
Emilii Medtner, circa 1910	126
Andrey Bely on a visit to the Medtners in 1911. From the left: Emilii, Nikolay, Anna, Bely, and pianist Nikolay Stember, Nikolay's pupil and second cousin.	127
From the left: psychiatrist Hans Trüb, Emma Jung, Emilii Medtner, Trüb's son Georg, and Jung on an outing to Alp Laui, Toggenburg in 1921.	133
Boris Pasternak, 1916.	136
Marietta Shaginyan, 1911.	140

Introduction

The Symbolists in Moscow and Petersburg in the early twentieth century dreamed of a new era that would fundamentally revolutionize the Russian way of life. These poets, philosophers, and mystics looked for signs in the sky, especially in radiant sunrises. They sensed that tsarist society was on the threshold of an apocalyptic upheaval. Before them they saw great syntheses led by Russia between Eastern and Western culture and among various art forms.

The Symbolists based themselves on Vladimir Solovyov and Friedrich Nietzsche. Solovyov had spoken in Gnostic terms of the World Soul that was attempting to break out of the prison of matter, of Sophia, the divine wisdom inherent in creation that the poets were summoned to find and give a name. Through his mouthpiece Zarathustra, Nietzsche had proclaimed the advent of a new age and called for rebellion against all conventional values.

Influences came from elsewhere as well. Like the "men of the 1860s" before them who had been awakened by Darwin and Marx, the Symbolists were impatient to see their new ideas translated into reality as soon as possible. Beneath their enormous ambitions was an unmistakable streak of Russian maximalism. They pinned their exorbitant expectations on the political revolution of 1905.

The circle around Andrey Bely in Moscow welcomed him as the modern Messiah when in 1902 he made his literary debut with an experiment in poetic prose emanating from his ecstatic visions during the first year of the new century. He aspired to nothing less than fusing his life with his art to become the harbinger of the great transformation.

Introduction

In the essays here I attempt to introduce the Symbolists and their feverish expectations in greater detail. Theirs was a time when for a brief moment everything seemed possible. Then came the rude awakening. It is described better than anywhere else in Bely's powerful prose masterpiece *Petersburg*, which serves as the connective thread and recurrent point of reference throughout the present collection. Written in the early 1910s just before the world war that was to culminate in the so-called October revolution, the novel portrays the collective experience of the Symbolists as an attempted political parricide.

These dreamers came back down to earth in different places. The experience had been so all-encompassing that it generated the need for a wide variety of powerful substitutes. There was enormous intellectual turbulence. Like Bely, some became Anthroposophists. One converted to Catholicism and another to Orthodoxy, and these two ended up as hybrid Catholic-Orthodox Uniates. Another evolved into a Stalinist and yet another became a Nazi.

The symptoms of the pathology were remarkably intertwined with Symbolist culture's rich artistic production. At the very moment of crisis, newly introduced depth psychology came to the rescue of some of the visionaries. In certain cases the result was a conceptual cross-fertilization, since the survivors of the calamity had a unique experience to communicate to their therapists.

Here as well there is a story.

Andrey Bely
and the Philosopher's Nephew

It is difficult to overstate the significance of the philosopher and poet Vladimir Solovyov's nephew Sergey for Andrey Bely. In his own memoirs, Bely calls it "colossal." The two men merged with and complemented each other. More and more, Sergey came to resemble Bely's double. Indeed, Sergey's maternal grandmother, Aleksandra Kovalenskaya, described them as two halves of a single personality. This relationship becomes especially clear when we consider Bely's literary figures, some of whom blend features of both.

They first met in late 1895, 15 and 10 years old, respectively. For the young Boris Bugaev (Bely's real name), the Solovyov family that had recently moved into the building in the Arbat in Moscow became an alternative or antithesis to the stifling reserve of his own family under the command of his professor father. He came to look upon publisher Mikhail Solovyov as a second father and Olga Solovyova, an artist, as a second mother. Albeit in different ways, both Mikhail and Olga were receptive to the new literary currents. In Sergey he found a surrogate brother who immediately was able to understand and respond to his improvised fantasies and play with symbols. Here in this family he was no longer tongue-tied and was allowed to express himself.

Around the turn of the century, "Borya's" and "Seryozha's" mutual mythmaking drew increasingly on Vladimir Solovyov's prophecies. It was thus that Bely's debut work, the prose poem *The Second Symphony (the Dramatic)*, emerged. When it was published in 1902, many in his intimate circle believed that the sixteen-year-old Sergey was the author. To some extent, in fact, he was, but he was also and equally the hero, a young mystic by the name of Sergey searching in passionate visions for the "Woman Clothed with the Sun," Solovyov's apocalyptic Sophia symbol. Bely later called his hero "a projection of the future Seryozha Solovyov."

It was Mikhail Solovyov who, on his own initiative, printed *The Second Symphony* with logotype borrowed from the publishing house Scorpio (The Scorpion) and gave the young debutant his pseudonym Andrey Bely—"Andrey the White." The work issued directly from Boris and Sergey's mystical rapture in the Arbat during the winter and spring of 1901. Their cult of dusk and dawn on the threshold of the new century and their ecstatic expectation of an approaching transformation of the world were rooted entirely in Vladimir Solovyov's poetry and philosophy. These sensations were so strong that they had a determining influence on their lives and writing—a point to which they constantly returned and in various forms attempted to interpret and recreate. In the fall of 1901, Bely began writing his third symphony, *The Return*, in which the Nietzschean abdication of reason that was perceptible as early as his first work became increasingly alluring. From the very beginning, Bely had been interested in psychiatry and mental border-crossings.

Sergey Solovyov, 1904.

In 1901 Sergey introduced Bely to the poetry of Aleksandr Blok (his second cousin), and in 1903 the two writers became personally acquainted. Blok's poetic invocations of a higher feminine principle seemed to concretize Bely's own expectations of the new century. At the same time, Mikhail Solovyov died, and his wife, who had for some time been psychologically unbalanced, shot herself. Sergey was forced to seek help from the well-known psychiatrist

Sergey Solovyov and Andrey Bely in Dedovo, 1905.

Ivan Sikorsky, who knew his relatives in Kiev. Soon Bely's father also passed away, thus linking Bely's fate once again to that of his friend.

When Bely was drawn into his great Petersburg drama with Aleksandr and Lyubov Blok amid the revolutionary ferment of 1904-1906, Sergey was the whole time at his side as a extremist instigator, urging him on much as in the games they used to play with symbols. They were both in love with Lyubov, the original object of Blok's Sophia cult. When Blok proved to be inadequate as both a theurgist and a husband, Bely attempted with Sergey's active assistance to take his place. The consequences were catastrophic, but they also had an extraordinarily stimulating impact on Bely's writing.

As for Sergey, now a philologist at Moscow University with an interest in antiquity, he fantasized about marrying a peasant girl as a revolutionary symbolic act. In the poetry he soon began publishing, he drew on his broad learning to interweave classical and Biblical motifs with Slavic folk mythology.

Bely's first prose work in a larger format, the novel *The Silver Dove*, harks back to his and Sergey's shared experience of the revolutionary mystique that culminated in 1906. The hero, the Symbolist poet Daryalsky, sallies out into the depths of the people and allies himself with a woman in a mystical sect on his mission to resurrect Russia. Besides reflecting Bely himself, he is modeled on Sergey to such a degree that when the latter became familiar with the writing of the novel, he even offered to pose for the role. Sergey was at the same time composing a prose work of his own with a similar theme, which, however, he never finished. In a poem written in January 1909, just as Bely was beginning the novel, he had addressed Sergey as his "beloved brother" and reminisced about their shared visionary ecstasy in 1901 and Russia's subsequent tribulations. The pair, the poem declared, were united by a force beyond the grave.

In the end, Sergey was understandably of two minds about the novel, and the first crack in their foster-brotherhood came into view. The rift surely also had to do with the fact that Sergey did not share Bely's (and Daryalsky's) affinity for occult doctrines.

In the fall of 1910, Bely began planning a new novel to be entitled *Petersburg*. It was another retrospective look at 1905-1906 and his desperate attempts to weave the Sophia cult into the Revolution. The theme of patricide in the work may have ultimately come from a talk Sergey had just held on the Oedipus motif in connection with a performance of *The Brothers Karamazov* at the Moscow Art Theater. Dramatizing reality as Symbolists were wont to do, Sergey was now active in Moscow's theatrical world. He had been dragged into a complicated and painful love affair with a woman with whom he had been close friends since childhood, the subsequently famous actress Sofya Giatsintova. The romance had a dramatically unhappy ending. Overwrought, he made a couple of suicide attempts and was admitted to a psychiatric clinic.

Sigmund Freud's psychoanalysis was making inroads in Russia around this time, not least in Sergey's environs at the Moscow University Clinic and at the sanatoria in Kryukovo and Podsolnechnoe near his family's summer home in Dedovo. In the winter of 1912 he underwent psychoanalysis by Dr. Yury Kannabikh at Kryukovo, which may make him the first writer in Europe to receive Freudian treatment.

Bely, whose heroes are constantly on the brink of mental breakdown, was in contact with Sergey's first physician in the fall of 1911 as he continued to work on *Petersburg*. These conversations doubtless gave him material for the novel, the basic theme of which, via the autobiographical relationship with his father and his conflict with Blok, is the destiny of Russia. The bomb thrower Dudkin—just like Sergey at the clinic—feels persecuted by an "oriental face" (that grows into his demon and destroyer of Russia, the chief terrorist Lippanchenko). And just like Sergey, Dudkin hovers on the verge of spiritual disintegration until his mind finally

Andrey Bely, 1916.

splits. Thus, albeit not as obviously as in *The Silver Dove*, in this case as well Sergey lends features to Bely's revolutionary activist characters. This does not become entirely clear until the end of the epilogue, when Senator Ableukhov's likewise mentally unstable son Nikolay (whose assassination plot has come to nothing) is reborn in the Russian countryside with Christlike physical features reminiscent of Sergey, who was now cured of his phobias. Just before finishing the novel, Bely had in fact met Sergey in Volhynia in the spring of 1913, in the company of his newly wedded wife Tatyana, the younger sister of Bely's unofficial wife Asya Turgeneva. At first, both he and Bely had been in love with Asya. Upon his release from Kryukovo, Sergey—in emulation of Bely—married the then merely sixteen-year-old Tatyana and set off on a honeymoon to Italy, as had Bely and Asya two years before.

Despite these imitations, in 1913 Bely and Sergey were moving away from each other again, and this second time the ideological gap was deeper. Sergey was increasingly involved with Orthodoxy, Byzantinism, and Slavophilism, and would eventually take holy orders, whereas Bely had already entered the newly founded Anthroposophical Society in Berlin. As Symbolism was now breaking down completely, both were in reality simply attempting in different ways to carry on Vladimir Solovyov's heritage.

After Bely's return from his long sojourn abroad with the Anthroposophists, they met again. In 1917 Bely lived off and on with his friend in Dedovo. The February Revolution inspired hopes in Sergey that the Eastern and Western Churches might be reunited, much in the spirit of Vladimir Solovyov. He spoke of a cosmic resurrection. After the October upheaval he wrote a thoroughly somber poem entitled "To My Friend Boris Bugaev" in which the perspective had undergone a drastic change. He now readied himself for humiliation and "stoning." He sought support from his friend, who at this moment was far less insightful than he (and who would soon, in the poem *Christ is Risen*, even interpret the revolutionary events in Aleksandr Blok's mystical spirit).

It was at this point that Sergey Solovyov's long passion really began. His marriage tragically dissolved in 1920, after which he again needed to seek psychiatric treatment. Like his uncle he converted to Catholicism, but after a few years of vacillation he went halfway back and joined the Uniate Church, which observes the Orthodox liturgy but is in communion with Rome. He lived a destitute and vulnerable life yet in addition to his activity as a priest, he was remarkably productive. He translated mostly classical authors from up to seven different languages, he wrote theological essays and finished a major monograph on his uncle— *Vladimir Solovyov's Life and Philosophical and Artistic Evolution*—in which Solovyov's East-West idea is central, as it always was to Moscow Symbolism.

To a large extent Bely lived retrospectively in the new Soviet state, writing memoirs in various forms and backward-looking novels. In May 1921 he wrote *The First Meeting*, a narrative poem that portrays the mystical transports of 1901, exactly twenty years before. The title itself plays on Vladimir Solovyov's poem "Three Meetings," about his three visions of Sophia. Central to Bely's work is his portrait of Sergey, which tersely captures his young friend's combined angelic and precocious personality.

Bely and Sergey went on meeting each other from time to time, and they continued to respect each other despite their utterly different ideological positions. On several occasions Bely spent the night in Sergey's spartanly furnished rented room in Moscow. In the summer of 1926, they met in Koktebel on the Black Sea. Toward the end of the decade both men became absorbed in writing memoirs about the early years. In 1930, Bely finished the first part of his reminiscences *On the Border of Two Centuries*, which concludes with a brilliant portrayal of Sergey and the mythmaking of their childhood and youth. Now, Bely writes, the two are united in an indestructible thirty-five-year-old friendship, even love (which was surely reinforced by their shared political difficulties). Bely was well aware that at the time Sergey was living dangerously. In 1929, the Communist Party had launched a violent anti-religious campaign. The small Catholic congregations had been dissolved, and Sergey had been forced to begin leading a kind of catacomb existence.

In February 1930, a little over a month after Bely finished *On the Border of Two Centuries*, the persecuted Sergey seems to have visited him in Kuchino outside Moscow. That he did so is evident from a poem Bely dedicated to him, characteristically entitled "To My Brother," the manuscript of which I obtained from Sergey's daughter Olga when I once met her in Moscow. This poem, written in Bely's typical broken verse lines, is yet another retrospective work. It portrays Sergey as akin to his uncle, a winged being from a different dimension. Ever since the turn-of-the-century Dionysian blizzard thirty years earlier in the magical year 1901, he had followed Bely like a blood relative, a mystical stimulus on both sight and sound. At this moment the two friends sense the approach of death, and Bely urges Sergei to lift his gaze to the heavens, where a star is dimly visible. It is not the Star of Bethlehem as in the *Second Symphony*, however, but instead a tear, their shared bitter experience. But soon they will find their Solovyovian "azure blue home," the eternity of their dreams. In a number of Vladimir Solovyov's poems—especially "Three Meetings," azure is linked to Sophia and a revealed reality beyond our own. Bely played on the connection as early as the title of his first poetry collection *Gold in Azure*: the golden sun against the azure blue sky.

Sergey Solovyov's days in freedom were numbered, and both he and Bely knew it. A few days later, on the night between 15 and 16 February 1930, he was apprehended in a wave of anti-Catholic arrests. Later that spring, Anthroposophists in Bely's circle, including his wife, were imprisoned. For the time being he was left alone.

In the GPU's interrogation rooms Sergey plunged once and for all into schizophrenia. He was paralyzed by feelings of guilt, believing he had poisoned the entire world. When Bely died in 1934, he was once again in a mental institution. He had intervals of lucidity but relapsed periodically into morbid passivity. He finally died in 1942 from self-imposed starvation after having been evacuated to Kazan early in the war. He was buried there in the middle of the bitterly cold winter, ironically enough—considering his own background—on the initiative of Evgeny Feinberg and Vitaly Ginzburg, two young physicists of a decidedly materialistic outlook. Feinberg was the brother of Sergey's son-in-law. Feinberg's friend Ginzburg, incidentally, would go on to be awarded the Nobel Prize in physics.

Symbolism integrated life and art. It was not least an experiment with fluid identities in which personalities—often with dramatic conflicts as a result—blurred into each other. Andrey Bely and Sergey Solovyov's "collective being" is an especially obvious example of the phenomenon, which lies at the very heart of Russian Symbolism.

Bely and Aleksandr Blok

*A*ndrey Bely's *Second Symphony (the Dramatic)* was born in the spring and summer of 1901. Of special significance to its fiery red visions of dawn is the mythologem of "the Woman Clothed with the Sun" from *Revelation* 12, who brings forth a man child who is to rule all nations with a rod of iron, vanquish the Beast, and save the world. In one of his three lectures in memory of Dostoevsky, Vladimir Solovyov had observed that the writer had been especially inclined to apply this apocalyptic symbolism to Russia and what he thought to be Russia's mission, namely, to bring forth the child of the dawn, the redeemer of the world. For Bely, these notions were closely tied to Nietzsche's "blond beast" of the new world.

Early in the fall of 1901, Sergey Solovyov introduced Bely to Aleksandr Blok's still unpublished poetic incantations. They made an enormous impression on him, and he increasingly set his hopes on this brother poet, of his same age, who appeared to be about to give a name to Sophia, the Divine Wisdom, the World-Mother. Blok seemed to have assumed the role of conjurer of the higher reality, an undertaking in keeping with Solovyov's notions of the verbal artist's new mission, which was to awaken the dormant World Soul. It was as though at this moment he was Bely's better self, someone who perhaps was capable of accomplishing what Bely was attempting but could not entirely manage.

Important in this context is the fact that Blok was in Petersburg, the site of the mighty visions of Aleksandr Pushkin, Nikolay Gogol, and Fyodor Dostoevsky. It was also Bely's mother's city, which she often contrasted with the academic Moscow milieu she did not like. Bely later reported that, initially, he imagined Blok standing on the banks of the Neva gazing into the sky. Here he quite emphatically links Blok to Pushkin's poem *The Bronze Horseman*, the point of departure for the entire Petersburg myth, with its apocalyptic keynote and famous apostrophe to Russia.

Blok and Bely's backgrounds seemed to have so much in common. Both were born in October 1880, both were sons of prominent university professors and had grown up in an academic environment, both were receptive to the new literary currents, and around the turn of the century they were equally impregnated with the philosophy of recently deceased Vladimir Solovyov. Bely's own mystical pretensions always encompassed a duality that included a satirical and self-mocking corrective. Blok seemed less ambiguous,

It took a while before they became personally acquainted. In the meantime Blok sent new poems to his second cousin Sergey that merely reinforced Bely's first impressions. Then something happened that both Bely and Blok came to regard as particularly significant. They sent letters to each other that evidently crossed in the mail and arrived simultaneously. Blok had been deeply impressed by "The Forms of Art," an article Bely had just published that commented philosophically on the new mysticism, and he, as the visionary, addressed some questions to Bely as the theoretical authority. As for Bely, in his letter he wanted to know more about Blok's cultic relationship with "Her." After this exchange they began corresponding intensively. In a way, they created a new genre in these letters, which were often very extensive and mingled personal messages, confessions, mystical exegesis, and drafts of literary works.

In the summer of 1903 Blok married Lyubov Mendeleeva, daughter of the creator of the periodic table of elements. Bely, informed and supported by Sergey, was already aware that it was she who was the object of Blok's cult poetry. He was himself invited to the wedding as an usher but was unable to attend due to his father's death and funeral. Sergey took his place and returned with ecstatic descriptions of the event as a cult ceremony in the service of his "Eternal Friend." Everything seemed to be charged with symbolism and significance. It was not for nothing that the bride's name was Lyubov, which means "love." The daughter of a great materialist,

Lyubov and Aleksandr Blok. 1903.

she appeared to be—to use yet another Solovyovian epithet—"the radiant daughter of dark chaos." As before, playfulness mixed with deep seriousness in the speculations of the young Moscow friends.

In early 1904, Bely and Blok finally met personally. Blok and his wife came to Moscow and were introduced to the young so-called Argonaut circle that had gathered around Bely. Expectations were so inflated and mutual projections so strong that both men were bound to be disappointed and perceive each other's physical presence as rather trivial. Blok even admitted that he found it difficult to converse with Bely. That summer they saw each other again when Bely and Sergey visited Blok at his summer home in Shakhmatovo, outside Moscow. Bely and Sergey were by this time so immersed in Blok's poetry that they both fell in love with Lyubov. Blok's first volume, *Verses on the Beautiful Lady*, whose title aroused associations with the chivalrous romance, came out later that fall. Bely's own poetry debut, a collection whose title *Gold in Azure* alluded, through Solovyov's solar incantations, to the color symbolism of icons of the Mother of God, appeared at about the same time. Bely and Sergey fantasized about future scholars finding traces of a "Blokist" sect—themselves, that is.

But something had happened. Blok had early on begun to have doubts about his poetry. The "She" of his visions seemed to be changing. He confessed in a personal conversation with Bely that he felt doom in his very genes, in what he had inherited from a demonic father figure who abandoned the family when he was just a baby. At the same time there were problems in his marriage. Bely was therefore all the more inclined to attempt to assume Blok's role as both the fore-singer of the new age and the worshipper of his wife. A love triangle on several levels became inevitable, and these tensions were heightened by dramatic current events. Just as Bely was leaving Shakhmatovo, the news came that the dreaded Minister of the Interior Plehve had been killed in the middle of Petersburg by a terrorist bomb.

Andrey Bely, 1904.

In January 1905, Bely came for the first time to Petersburg to visit the Bloks. Remarkably enough, his arrival happened to coincide with Bloody Sunday, the prelude to the revolutionary events of that year, which were also a direct consequence of Russia's devastating defeat in the naval war with Japan. The tsarist regime was shaken, and the resounding mystical ecstasy Bely experienced at the turn of the century took on an increasingly political significance. Lyubov Blok seemed to respond positively to his feelings. In the spring he published an article on "The Apocalypse in Russian Poetry" in which he argued that nineteenth-century poets up to Solovyov had attempted to capture the contours of Sophia, the World Soul, and that at this crucial moment the Symbolists were about to accomplish the mission by liberating "the Woman Clothed with the Sun" and thereby freeing the nation from its shackles.

As the revolutionary process was approaching its climax in August, Bely wrote "The Green Meadow," an article in which he applied the symbolism of Gogol's "A Terrible Vengeance" to Russia's predicament. In Gogol's story, Katerina is tightly bound to her diabolical sorcerer father. She remembers her carefree childhood full of circle dancing and games on "the meadow so green." Bely

Aleksandr Blok, 1907.

summons Katerina-Russia to free herself from oppression and re-create her pleasant past. On another level he is quite simply beseeching Lyubov Blok to leave her marriage. Later he described this essay as a love letter with specific associations that went over the heads of his readers. Soon after, he made a couple more trips to Petersburg. Without telling Blok in so many words, he hinted in murky fantasies about moving in with them in a new ménage a trois that would be a kind of anarchic mini-commune. When the Revolution was bloodily crushed in the late fall and the tsarist repression took hold, in Bely's view these events were increasingly linked with Lyubov's still strong ties to Blok, who now seemed prepared to question everything he had once professed. Bely had just become acquainted with Blok's newly written play *The Puppet Show*, in which he had been so bold as to portray himself and Bely as Harlequin and Pierrot and the dream of transforming the world as a farce. Such a drastic dethroning of the earlier ambitions of both men could only serve to intensify the provocation.

In the spring of 1906, Bely drew closer to Lyubov. He dreamed of running away with her to another mythical city of water and canals: Venice. But she withdrew, and once she had made her decision it was irrevocable. Bely's maniacally complex attitudes had played a role. He was capable of at one and the same time dispatching eight letters to Lyubov, three to Blok, and one to Blok's mother, many of them contradictory. Toward the end of the summer he desperately challenged Blok to a duel (which was not taken seriously), entertained feverish notions of joining the terrorists, and, as he openly admitted to his friend Emilii Medtner, had perversely detailed fantasies of murder. It seemed to Bely's inner eye that Blok, who had abandoned his theurgic mission and now gave himself up instead to drinking and brothels, was drifting into the overt cynicism of the tsarist regime. In his poetry and dramatic works Blok had even begun to debase the Cosmic Feminine, degrading Her as a Petersburg prostitute. Here there was a satirical dialectic with which Bely himself had never been unfamiliar and which had appeared in his very first published work. It all was too much, however. Bely fled abroad for six months, not to Venice but to the artistic milieus of Munich and Paris.

As decadence took hold of Petersburg in the form of so called "Mystical Anarchism," which (with Blok on the periphery of the movement) transformed mysticism into pure eroticism, Bely began working through his dramatic experiences. They provided abundant materials for his Dionysian poem in prose, *A Goblet of Blizzards: Fourth Symphony*, as well as an entire poetic suite significantly entitled *Ashes* into which his personal drama is interwoven, and some initial attempts at prose. Not least these latter endeavors contained cheeky, provocative allusions to the mysterious love triangle that was now debased and parodied as in Blok's recent works, with jabs at both the deposed theurgist and his deceitful "World Soul," which Bely, obviously alluding to Blok's play, later characterized in his memoirs as a self-centered puppet.

As soon as he returned home from abroad, Bely threw himself into a furious polemic with literary Petersburg. Pushkin, Gogol, and Dostoevsky's city had become a literary swamp, the site of a conspiracy against Russian verbal art basically aimed at all of Russia herself. Diabolical forces had taken over and profaned the sacred. It was moreover quite clear that Blok was the key figure in these vehement and extravagant diatribes, which of course also harked back to the ancient quarrel between "genuinely Russian" Moscow and the false, gaudy facades of "imported" Petersburg. Finally, Bely ceased beating about the bush and launched a satirical frontal attack against Blok in an article entitled "The Detritus of Worlds," mocking him as the bard of corruption and decay, a poet whose verses were as spongy as a French cheese.

Almost everything Bely wrote during this period seems related in various ways to his personal drama. It soon became apparent that the prose pieces were merely a prelude to a novel, *The Silver Dove*, in which the love triangle is set in a national Russian frame. The plot of the work centers on the Symbolist poet Daryalsky, who becomes entangled in a flagellant sect headed by the mysterious, hypnotic Kudeyarov and the sensual peasant woman Matryona, the "Mother of God" of the group, who, together with Daryalsky, is called upon to give birth to the savior of Russia. Daryalsky ultimately becomes a victim of the sectarians' demonic intrigues.

But there was more to come. In 1910 the two brethren poets reconciled and became as deeply attached to each other as before. Bely gave a lecture in Moscow on Dostoevsky as a national visionary, to which Blok was, symbolically enough, personally invited. After that, Bely set off abroad on an informal honeymoon with the new woman in his life, Ivan Turgenev's cousin's granddaughter Asya, named after the eponymous heroine of one of Turgenev's short stories. To Bely she represented something different from Lyubov Blok, namely the gentle pride of Turgenev's character. In fact, in *The Silver Dove* she lent some of her features to a cool opposite of the disastrous Matryona. From this trip, which ended in Egypt, Bely returned with a mental outline of *Petersburg* that finally seemed to process his experiences. The apocalyptic city had become a hellish phantom scene and Sophia the Divine Wisdom was reduced to shallow little Sofya Likhutina, a new caricature of Lyubov Blok. It is in fact Sofya's whimsical behavior that seems to trigger the young Nikolay Ableukhov's patricidal instinct and revolutionary nightmares.

Thus Blok becomes the axis of Bely's entire oeuvre. He continues in that capacity in Bely's subsequent post-Symbolist retrospective phase as well, for in his reminiscences Bely bases himself on an extensive and uniquely detailed portrait of what at that point in the early 1920s was his recently deceased "better half," who had been transformed into his "worse half" to be scourged and ruthlessly exploited for the sake of artistic satire. The memoir phase as well, in fact, divides into two Blok sections. In the first, in *Reminiscences of Blok*, Bely sorrowfully and regretfully praises him as a poetic witness to the age. In the second, in the last part of his memoir trilogy *Between Two Revolutions*, ten years later, he once again ridicules and showers him with disappointment. Thus Aleksandr Blok can be said to carry Bely's oeuvre in various ways, for without the great Symbolist poet Bely would have written scarcely any really significant prose.

The Symbolist with Two Careers

Lev Kobylinsky's works can be divided neatly into two parts: his writings published during his Symbolist period under the pseudonym Ellis, and works written in emigration under the signature Dr. Leo Kobilinski-Ellis. In fundamental respects they are polar opposites, and have generally been treated separately. Lev Kobylinsky has been described as a biographical riddle, a man who pursued two distinct artistic careers in two different countries and languages. I shall attempt to show that there was in fact continuity and inherent logic in this seemingly schizophrenic double oeuvre.

Let us briefly review the basic background facts. Ellis was active in Russia, while Dr. Kobilinski (as I choose to call him for simplicity's sake) worked in Italian Switzerland. Ellis wrote in Russian, Dr. Kobilinski in German. Ellis was above all a poet and critic, while Dr. Kobilinski was a literary and cultural scholar active in introducing Russian culture to Europe. Just as Marina Tsvetaeva describes him in her poem *The Sorcerer,* Ellis was a Symbolist anarchist, agitator, and eccentric visionary. He was an extraordinarily influential source of ideas and impulses, not least for Andrey Bely, for whom he seems to have assumed the role of double and omnipresent shadow around 1907. Night was his element, and he openly celebrated madness and psychic duality. The world was but a dead cadaver, life but a shadow reality. The artist was called to be a theurgist who evoked another reality through symbols, and, because he lived in dreams and fantasies, was a madman and buffoon in the eyes of the world. The artist must with his entire being welcome social upheaval, and even—as Ellis proclaimed around 1905—revolutionary terror. Memoirists unanimously describe him as Mephistophelian. Such an attitude made sense within his Gnostic worldview, for since the world was in the hands of the demiurge, he chose in various contexts to play along and conjure forth demonic forces.

In contrast, Dr. Kobilinski in exile had a mystical confidence in this world, and worked in silence and meditation to build bridges over cultural rifts and conflicts. Most of all he wanted to bring to the West Vladimir Solovyov's dream of reconciling and reuniting the Eastern and Western Churches. His guiding light was the idea of All-Unity that posited the world as a mystical totality. It was probably no coincidence that in exile Lev Kobylinsky—with no real basis—chose to call himself "Doctor," for it was a title that suggested both erudition and a therapeutic mission to heal the wounded twentieth century. Where Ellis had been a specter wandering around nocturnal Moscow, a Symbolist outsider in an alien world, Dr. Kobilinski lived in a house that basked in the sunlight on the Mountain of the Trinity (Monti della Trinità) near the famous medieval Franciscan monastery Madonna del Sasso and had a splendid view over Lake Maggiore. Mentally, at least, Dr. Kobilinski appears to have joined the Uniate Church, which observes Orthodox ritual but is in communion with Catholicism.

It took Lev Kobylinsky ten years to make the changeover and completely switch roles. In the fall of 1911 he suddenly left Russia and became a follower of "spiritual scientist" Rudolf Steiner. In the spring of 1914, he published as Ellis his second and last collection of poetry, *Argot*, in Moscow. He returned in his new guise in 1924.

To put it drastically, Lev Kobylinsky traveled from Satan to God, from playing with darkness to deepest piety. He is not entirely unique in this respect, for his evolution displays at least certain structural similarities with another Symbolist poet, namely Aleksandr Dobrolyubov. In the 1890s, Dobrolyubov's activities included participation in satanic masses, but subsequently he took St. Francis's naïve and life-affirming outlook as his ideal and lived a pious life among his own sect out in the countryside. Another who springs to mind to some degree is the Dadaist Hugo Ball, who as a convert to Catholicism in the 1920s turned to the devout asceticism of Eastern Christianity and the Byzantine Fathers of the

The Symbolist with Two Careers

Lev Kobylinsky (Ellis). 1897.

Lev Polivanov.

Church. Although they both lived in Switzerland, Dr. Kobilinski had no contact with Ball. Dobrolyubov's example, however, was both important and relevant as Russian Symbolism entered its crisis after 1910.

How was Kobylinsky's dramatic metamorphosis possible? The key may lie in his relationship to his father, Lev Polivanov, who seems to have played a crucial role in both phases of his life.

Polivanov was a prominent literary scholar and brilliant pedagogue who headed his own *gymnasium*, or secondary school, with Andrey Bely among his enthusiastic pupils. He also translated and published textbooks. A Slavophile and friend of Vladimir Solovyov and Fyodor Dostoevsky, he eventually developed a philosophy of unity that bore a certain kinship to Solovyov's. He was married and had several children. Suddenly, in the mid-1870s a young tutor, Varvara Kobylinskaya, came into the family, and Polivanov began a liaison with her. She gave birth to a son, Ilya, in 1876. Lev was born three years later, in 1879. To his wife's horror, Polivanov was now a bigamist with two families.

In June 1880, Polivanov organized the huge Pushkin Celebration in Moscow coinciding with the unveiling of the statue dedicated to the poet. Dostoevsky delivered his classic Pushkin speech honoring the poet for striving toward unity, the example he set as a bridge between cultures, and his "universal humanity." The next day Polivanov's wife sought out Dostoevsky and asked for his support and guidance in her family drama. What she told him was in glaring contrast to the message of Dostoevsky's speech and the notion of organic unity that he and Polivanov shared. Desperate, she informed him of her husband's betrayal and duplicity and his basic inability and even unwillingness to address the problem. It is clear from the subsequent correspondence between her and Dostoevsky that she had made a strong impression on him. He was in the middle of writing *The Brothers Karamazov*, and it may well be that the Polivanov family drama has left its mark on the novel. Dostoevsky died some six months later.

Lev Kobylinsky spent his first years of life in the early 1880s in a situation in which the two women were evidently unwilling to surrender Polivanov. Another illegitimate son, Sergey, was born in 1882. It can be presumed that both families were in constant turmoil. In the end, Polivanov appears to have chosen to leave Kobylinskaya and devote himself exclusively to his large first family, a decision that cut off the three Kobylinsky brothers from their father and half-siblings and forced them to live in straitened material circumstances. From these early years, Kobylinsky took with him a dual inheritance of turbulence, bitterness, and sorrow mixed with fantasies and dream projects as a means of relief and escape. His father died in 1899.

Ellis the Symbolist had no family: he had no contact with Ilya and was estranged from his mother (who died before her time in 1907) and his younger brother Sergey. He hid the fact that he was Polivanov's son from all but his closest friends. With no permanent home, he lived in a room in a central Moscow boarding house. He climbed all the barricades, behaved provocatively and indulged his childishness, touchiness, and neuroses. He may have had an Oedipal complex.

A letter Ellis wrote in 1912 indicates that this rebel and mischief-maker possessed a surprisingly large measure of self-insight. There he describes himself as childish, naïve, maximalist and unbalanced, ruthlessly subjective and egoistic—a pose deliberately adopted by a man whose life he says was "smashed to pieces" in his early childhood. This self-characterization came shortly before he declared, in the foreword to his 1913 collection of poetry *Argot*, that it was natural for the modern poet to indulge in the voices, spectral visions, dreams, and tales of childhood—the one true, imperishable reality we have that can be interpreted only by those who have preserved the child within. One of the aims of the introductory section is to reawaken the "little lost Paradise," much as Symbolism as a whole was in his view called upon to reawaken and give form to the "great lost Paradise." This first section in *Argot* consists of 27 poems that are either about or dedicated to children. Some of them, like Teresa of Avila, have glowing visions, but others are abandoned, desperately yearning, and sobbing.

Thus, in both his life and his art, Ellis the Symbolist chose to hold on to the child's view of the world, declaring that this was a genuinely Russian trait. It was Russians who had preserved the child within. Ellis, Bely concludes in *The Beginning of the Century*, the second part of his memoir trilogy, describes him as a "helpless, irresponsible, sick child" who would sometimes cry out at night, haunted by recurrent nightmares of "monsters" trying to "smother" him. Thus he can be said to have had two childhoods: the real one that had been "smashed to pieces" and was full of unrelieved sorrow, and one that was a flight from reality consisting of dreams, fantasies, fairy tales, and wonderful projections. Early on, he realized that the world is cruel and merciless, and that only intangible visions manifested in poetry and art give it meaning. It is there, between these two poles of suffocating memories and liberating visions, that his works seem to move.

This becomes particularly clear in Symbolism's late phase. In 1909, Ellis wrote *The Tightrope Dancer*, a play for children set in the circus. The protagonist was once abducted from a sheltered life with his affluent parents, but he does not know that. He has only memories of a happy, winged life in a fairy-tale world. His friend, the weeping "snake-boy," was sold by his father to the circus and has terrible memories of constant conflicts between his mother

Leonid Pasternak's sketch of Ellis (Lev Kobylinsky), Nikolay Berdyaev and Andrey Bely attending a lecture by Vyacheslav Ivanov in 1910.

and father and the devastating emotional chill that permeated his early years. Here the vision and the shadow world are side by side—childhood as both paradise and hell—the dual concept that perhaps underlay Kobylinsky's entire commitment to Symbolism. Also in 1909, Ellis delivered a lecture entitled "The Laughing Man" at the big Gogol Celebration in Moscow, in which he drew parallels between the "laughing man" (Gwymplaine in Victor Hugo's novel *The Laughing Man*) who was sold at the age of two and transformed into a tragic circus freak, and Gogol, "the crying man," whose agony similarly began "in his early years."

Bely's *Petersburg*, which was written during the time after 1910 when Ellis was moving from Symbolism to Steiner's Anthroposophy, seems to be strongly colored by Ellis's experiences. The rebels in the novel inhabit a thoroughly split shadow world. They suffer from convulsions and nightmare visions rooted in their own childhoods. Nikolay Ableukhov comes to regard the bomb with which he is to assassinate his father as the materialization of something chaotically infantile within his own emotional life. Even the instigator of the terror, Lippanchenko, is described as a hurt child who "cries out in his sleep."

Steiner was in reality only a transitional phase for Ellis. After prostrating himself at the feet of the "Master," in a polemical pamphlet entitled *Vigilemus!* he vehemently took issue with what he had just recently praised. After a few years of silence he reappeared on the European cultural scene as a Russian proponent of unity. Living now in a platonic relationship with the Dutch medium Johanna van der Meulen, he had settled down in a Roman and Catholic cultural environment and had been reconciled with the father whose love he had been denied, evidently having internalized his father—the Pushkinist, but also the Romanist—in his personality. It was not for nothing that they had the same first name.

Dr. Kobilinski's message was reconciliation itself in the broad sense. In the 1920s and 1930s, much like his old friend Sergey Solovyov, he attempted to bring Vladimir Solovyov's legacy to life for a Western audience, translating and introducing his poetry as well as his philosophical essays. His effort toward unity took place on two levels simultaneously, both in what he practiced and what he preached, as he described in German a Russian dream of wholeness that was intended to heal a divided Christianity. He eventually devoted his energies in several German-speaking countries to presenting and deepening knowledge about medieval Russian mysticism and the Byzantine intellectual heritage—everything connected with the idea of Holy Russia.

Concurrent with this activity, Dr. Kobilinski followed up on his father's pedagogical and literary scholarship with two monographs on Vasily Zhukovsky and Pushkin, publishing in 1933 *V. A. Zhukovsky: His Personality, His Life, and His Oeuvre*, a three-hundred page work in German dedicated to Vladimir Solovyov on the occasion of the 150th anniversary of the poet's birth. Twice as long, his father's major opus on Zhukovsky's life and work had appeared in 1883 on the 100th anniversary.

Why was Vasily Zhukovsky so important to both father and son? Well, because in the spirit of Romanticism his dual vision had captured two worlds—earthly and heavenly reality—in harmony with each other. Universalist and ecumenical in outlook, he was an interpreter of the poetry of different countries, a bridge between East and West and a pioneer who paved the way for Russia's national poet. Another factor important to Lev Kobylinsky was that Zhukovsky had focused especially on German-speaking Europe and finally settled in Germany. He had traveled in Switzerland and even visited Lake Maggiore.

Most significant of all, however, was that Zhukovsky was himself born out of wedlock as the illegitimate son of a rich Russian landowner and a Turkish woman abandoned by his father, who died a premature death. In the first pages of the monograph, Polivanov traces Zhukovsky's romantic melancholy to his abnormal childhood. Dr. Kobilinski refers to the passage in a footnote, quoting the poet's mournful cry in italics: *"Ah, if only I had had a father!"* Perhaps Lev Kobylinsky was able to convince himself that his father's monograph, which was written in his own early childhood, had begun as a working through of a trauma in which he projected his guilt for his absence during his son's early years onto Zhukovsky. Dr. Kobilinski emphasizes that Zhukovsky was born in the middle of a family quarrel but was able to transform his unhappy origins into a message of reconciliation.

The structure and presentation of Dr. Kobilinski's book is closely patterned on the intimate intertwining of life and poetry in his father's enormous study. The fact that his father concealed himself behind a pseudonym may have made this compliance even easier. Occasionally he quotes this "Zagarin," and sometimes he borrows phrasings and expressions without acknowledging the source. Presumably, he felt he was entitled to such liberties for several reasons. Perhaps there was a connection with the role of child he was playing. In a number of biographical respects he—like a child—could permit himself to lie. He was of course not a doctor. He included books in his vita that had never been published. He groundlessly claimed to have taught at an institution of higher learning, and in all his official documents he added five years to his real age.

Before moving on from Zhukovsky to Pushkin, Dr. Kobilinski wrote an article on Gogol originally entitled "The Power of Crying and Laughing. On the Emotional History of N. Gogol," published in two installments in 1937 and 1938. The road Gogol the writer followed, he noted in an echo of his remarks on the same topic 30 years earlier in Moscow, led to the demonic, mocking laughter that brought Gogol the man to tears and ruin. Ravaged by the anguish that had plagued him "from childhood," Gogol literally wept as he approached the end of his life.

Much like his work on Zhukovsky, Dr. Kobilinski's monograph on Pushkin, *Aleksandr Pushkin: Russia's Religious*

Genius, which was published posthumously in Switzerland in 1948, reflects the erudition of Polivanov's extensively annotated five-volume collection of Pushkin's works, the first of its kind in Russia. Announced as an edition intended "for family and classroom," it appeared in 1887, when Lev Kobylinsky was a young child. Echoing Dostoevsky's famous speech and Vladimir Solovyov's interpretation, Dr. Kobilinski describes Pushkin as a split genius who, despite his sorrowful and loveless childhood, was a religious poet who resolved the contradictions of Russian life by fusing with the soul of the Russian people. His "universal humanity," the concluding lines suggest, paved the way for Vladimir Solovyov's ecumenism.

Especially in *Boris Godunov*, the work on which both Dr. Kobilinski and his father focus particular attention, Pushkin's "divinely childlike naïveté" gave powerful expression to the tragedy of the Russian soul. Pushkin's greatness manifests itself in his portrayals of vulnerable children—as for example in his epitaph to Nikolay Volkonsky, the abandoned and "undeservedly" suffering little son of the Decembrist's wife Mariya Volkonskaya. It culminates in his portrait of the tsarevich Dimitry in *Boris Godunov*, in which the "angelic" child acquires the stature of a holy martyr and is the real main protagonist and hub of this colossal national drama.

There is consistency in Lev Kobylinsky's evolution—a link connecting his two bodies of work. The officially unacknowledged, rebellious illegitimate son finds the path leading to his Slavophile father's universalism, a path that takes him both to medieval Holy Russia, where the distance between heaven and earth was short, and to the roots of Russian literature in the Romantic heritage and the national poet's healing and harmonizing influence.

Symbolism's Charlatan

The unmasking in February 1909 of Evno Azef, a sophisticated double-agent organizer of terrorist assassinations, caused a change of mentality in Russia, for it marked the definitive end of the dreams of radical social transformation that in 1905 had briefly seemed to the Symbolists to embody their vision of a national spiritual regeneration. Now idealism yielded to resignation, open cynicism, and ideological confusion.

The unmasking at about the same time of Valentin Sventsitsky as a charlatan with ties to Symbolist circles (where terrorism had been held in high regard), did not, of course, have the same consequences for society, but it deeply impacted people around him. Mark Vishnyak writes in his memoirs that some—Vishnyak himself included—never recovered from the shock.

Valentin Sventsitsky's radical mystique had roots in Dostoevsky, Vladimir Solovyov, and Ibsen. He was especially close to a fellow student with similar interests, Vladimir Ern. Immediately after Bloody Sunday, in January 1905, he, accompanied by Ern, appeared in Petersburg. His visit had a very specific purpose, which was to found the so-called Christian Brotherhood of Struggle, an organization that was to spread revolution to the narrow-minded Church and, in brief, to fuse Orthodoxy with a combination of anarcho-socialism and Solovyovianism. Speculations on how man could become Solovyov's God-man alternated with discussions of trade-union rights. Sventsitsky came into contact with Dmitry Merezhkovsky and Zinaida Gippius's Religious-Philosophical Society in Petersburg, which for the most part aspired to bring about the same fundamental change in the Church. The ultimate goal of his and Ern's trip was to appeal to the Russian bishops and try to take their revolutionary agenda all the way to the Holy Synod, which was governed by the arch-reactionary Pobedonostsev. This was in fact the first attempt ever to formulate a socio-political doctrine within the Orthodox Church; it was even noted by Lenin in Switzerland in his newspaper *Vperyod* (*Forward*).

During the Revolution of 1905-1906, Sventsitsky became feverishly active. He gave fiery speeches, he set up an illegal printing press, he spread proclamations, leaflets, and appeals (which were always imprinted with a black cross, the symbol of the Christian Brotherhood), he threw himself into debates. Those who knew him attested to his exceptional charisma. Several observers have noted his hypnotic power over others, using terms such as "magnetism" and "magic" to describe the allure of his fiery gaze and suggestively soft voice. He enchanted his listeners and was soon surrounded by a growing band of proselytes. In 1906, he founded a Religious-Philosophical Society in Moscow. The topic he especially emphasized in his speeches and articles was the question of love and violence — how to reconcile Christian belief with the need for political violence in the struggle to liberate the people. He wrote prayers for executed assassins. He canonized bombers as saints and expiated vaguely and ambiguously upon "terror and immortality." He thought it legitimate to resort to violence, at least in strikes, in order to "restrain the greed" of oppressors and exploiters. He seemed to conquer all his opponents with his intelligence, his rhetorical fervor, and his uncompromising moralism (Vishnyak, who was a political activist at the time and later a prominent émigré intellectual, calls him in his memoirs "perhaps the most naturally talented person I have ever met"). He was implacable in his repudiation and condemnation of priests and theologians whose course differed from his own. He ordained self-mortification and a strict "Eastern Christian" asceticism, and himself lived like a monk in a simple cell with a cross on the wall. On a visit to him, Bely once discovered weapons in his spartanly furnished room. Bely even reports in his memoirs that Sventsitsky was preparing to assassinate a prominent tsarist functionary with a bomb, but did not manage to fulfill the mission.

At this time Sventsitsky was ubiquitous. He held forth among writers and philosophers at the Religious-Philosophical Society, where he also attempted to found what was called "a free theological university." He appeared with the Symbolists at the Society for Free Aesthetics and was a member, together with Bely, on the board of the Literary-Artistic Circle. He contributed to Nikolay Berdyaev and Sergey Bulgakov's journal *Voprosy zhizni* (*Questions of Life*). Together with Ern he sponsored and wrote for journals such as *Voprosy religii* (*Questions of Religion*), *Zhivaya zhizn* (*The Living Life*), and *Vek* (*The Century*). He contributed to the Symbolist anthology *Svobodnaya sovest* (*A Free Conscience*). He started several short-lived publications that were closed by the authorities. He initiated a popular series of booklets on religious and political issues. He published pamphlets with the anarchist house Trud i Volya (Labor and Liberty).

In his memoirs Andrey Bely associates Sventsitsky in these years with the cross and the bomb. Sventsitsky is reported to have spoken of fire from the heavens as a bomb that the great prophets attempted to bring down to earth, the very synthesis of original Christianity's radicalism and social protest à la Aleksandr Herzen. Now the historic moment had come for it to explode. Just as for Bely, the bomb assumed symbolic dimensions. The idea in Bely's own neo-Kantian hair-splitting was that the bomb created new values by dissipating the stagnation and inertia of life.

An entire generation of Russian intellectuals had come to idealize bomb-throwing and its resultant death and destruction. In the space of four years there were over 4,000 attacks on persons of authority. In early 1907, Sventsitsky delivered an overwrought lecture at the Religious-Philosophical Society about the maximalism of Ibsen's character Brand, whom he held up as a necessary model for Russians. Soon, however, he was overcome by remorse and misgivings, and the ideological retreat began. In December that same year, Sventsitsky suddenly published his Dostoevskian novel *The Antichrist*, whose subtitle *Notes of a Strange Man* and autobiographical allusions provide a clear glimpse of the double balance sheet he had been keeping and his secret betrayal of everything for which he had so fanatically agitated. Fear of death rules the hero of the novel. He feels he is serving the Antichrist, that he harbors the devil within himself. He considers Christ to be a lie, a false superstructure erected on humanity's collective dread of dying.

Valentin Sventsitsky, 1910s.

He repeats Sventsitsky's political evolution, urging the bishops to become active politically and founding an underground Christian combat organization. He mercilessly condemns the weak in spirit, but his uncompromising moralizing is shown to issue from his own anxiety. He abandons his pious female consort to indulge in sexual excesses with a peasant girl. His former companion is accidentally shot to death during political disturbances, a reference to the revolutionary events of the fall of 1905, and the hero takes refuge in a bordello. *The Antichrist* belongs to the candidly cynical literature of retribution that was typical of the period; it has features in common, for example, with Mikhail Artsybashev's markedly nihilistic novel *Sanin*.

After the novel Sventsitsky's position was no longer the same. In November 1908 the Religious-Philosophical Society he himself had founded took the unprecedented step of expelling him. It was in precisely the same month that the radical journalist Vladimir Burtsev began to unravel Azef's double-dealing, and a few weeks later he made his findings public. Sventsitsky had not been in the service of the tsarist police in his political activities, and he had revealed his duplicity himself, openly admitting his novel's autobiographical background in a foreword to the second edition. Azef's betrayal was obviously greater and had quite different consequences. And yet they both were kindred chameleons who, behind their heroic public personae, sought above all to satisfy their own desires and needs. It is remarkable that their charisma was so powerful that those who were most directly affected by their duplicity were not fully capable of exposing it. Boris Savinkov appeared almost incapable of understanding how Azef had deceived him over the years. The religious philosopher Sergey Bulgakov, who for a time belonged to

Sventsitsky's Christian Brotherhood and was entirely captivated by him, expressed remorse and hesitation after the expulsion.

Both Sventsitsky and Azef were inveterate liars. They knew how to use their almost hypnotic powers of persuasion to play on the feelings of others. Witnesses unanimously agree that they seemed able to cry at will, and they were cunningly skillful at interlarding their tyrannical stratagems with unctuous self-pity. As has been suggested by various observers, both may have been spiritually empty and devoid of an authentic personal identity.

What was it, then, that was revealed about Sventsitsky and that was to some extent evident already in *The Antichrist*? At the same time that he was parading his extreme asceticism and showering those around him with curses, he was wallowing in sexual debauchery, both on the estate near the monastery and in his own cell. There were rumors of erotic orgies. It was known that he had seduced young admirers one after the other. He also got three of them pregnant. The story has it that the three remained good friends. He betrayed and deceived everyone around him. On one occasion he was solemnly seen off and cheered at a Moscow train station as he departed for Macedonia to join a group of young rebels fighting the Ottoman Empire. But it was all just theater—he never arrived there, and the incident occurs in his novel as well. The ascetic was an erotomaniac who took what he wanted; the revolutionary, the prophet who wanted to bring the fires of heaven down to the earth, was an egotistic hedonist who went out into the countryside instead of leading the struggle in Macedonia to demonstrate Orthodox solidarity. It was as though all four of the brothers Karamazov were living within him. Sergey Bulgakov, in fact, commented on this with a paraphrase of Mitya Karamazov's conversation with Alyosha: "Man is too complicated. I'd have him simpler."

Sventsitsky had many lives. After a cleverly orchestrated flight to France, in 1909 he reappeared in a new guise. Among other contexts in a polemic with Vasily Rozanov, he proclaimed that sin and deceit were the inescapable precondition for penance and salvation, the only path to deeper self-knowledge. Here there is an argument that clearly resembles the Flagellants' notion of the orgiastic path to spirituality, an idea that was being illustrated at exactly this time in *The Silver Dove*. Sventsitsky now also turned to Ibsen's theme of living a lie in two connected dramas—*Death* and *Pastor Relling*. The latter play, which contains direct allusions to Ibsen, was staged by Pavel Orlenev at his theater. The hero in both, the young Pastor (not Ibsen's Doctor) Relling, is obsessed with his fear of death and his sexuality—his superior seduction techniques—and is driven to suicide.

The resurrected Sventsitsky lay behind the formation of a new group, the so called Golgotha Christians, whose ideology had much in common with that of the 1905 Christian Brotherhood. They advocated the same national rebirth, but now with even more emphasis on the cross and Golgotha. They similarly aspired to integrate Heaven and Earth, Orthodoxy and Socialism, the intelligentsia and the people, and to make the early Christian idea of brotherhood a social reality. They founded a journal first titled *Novaya Zemlya* (*The New Earth*) and then renamed *Novoe Vino* (*The New Wine*). At the same time Sventsitsky published *The Intelligentsia*, another self-examination in dramatic form that reflected his new commitments; in it, a writer rejects the falsehood of his revolutionary plans for liberation and embarks on a spiritual quest out into the depths of the people. At this point, Sventsitsky was no longer collaborating with Ern and Bulgakov, but with the defrocked priest Iona Brikhnichyov, who had been involved earlier as the representative of the Christian Brotherhood of Struggle in Tiflis. Among Brikhnichyov's fellow students at the seminary was Iosif Dzhugashvili, who gained fame as a revolutionary under the name Stalin. In his poems, Brikhnichyov praised Sventsitsky as the herald of a new age. Ten years later—after secularizing his dream of resurrection and becoming a propagandist of atheism—he took Dzhugashvili as his inspiration, writing grandiloquent letters addressed to Joseph Stalin in the Kremlin vowing his commitment to Soviet society.

Thus when Bely began writing *Petersburg* in the fall of 1911, Azef was no longer on the scene, whereas Sventsitsky had returned in a new role. Bely combines the two of them—with their similar traits—in his portrait of the repulsive, double-dealing terrorist leader Lippanchenko. One can, if one wishes, view Lippanchenko as the real chief protagonist of the novel. In the end he is killed by the bomb-thrower Dudkin. This murder is to some extent modeled on the Socialist Revolutionaries' bloody retaliation in 1906 against the unmasked tsarist agent Father Gapon, who had led the crowd of demonstrating workers on Bloody Sunday.

Bely claims in his memoirs that he tended to see through Sventsitsky from the outset, and that early on he was nauseated by his filthy and smutty appearance, which seemed to betray an inner treacherousness. This is probably not the whole truth. In fact, in the late summer of 1908 in Petersburg Bely chose to dedicate "The Motherland," one of his most important poems, to Sventsitsky. Appearing in his 1909 collection *Ashes*, it contains the subsequently famous stanza "Ill-fated land, ice-bound,/Cursed with an iron fate—/ Mother Russia, o wicked mother/Who has mocked thee thus?" This all happened only shortly before Sventsitsky was unmasked. At the same time, it is a fact—not a detail added by Bely—that Sventsitsky was not very attentive to his personal hygiene. Mark Vishnyak, who even 50 years later in his memoirs admits Sventsitsky's enormous influence on him and for the most part expresses respect for him, writes that from his school years and on through adult life Sventsitsky always had dirty black fingernails.

There is no escaping the fact that frauds are a particularly frequent theme in Russian literature. The chief precursor, of course, was Gogol, and Merezhkovsky had shown in his monograph how Gogol had struggled with his false roles and how his innate diabolism seems to have crushed him as he was working on *Dead Souls*. As Merezhkovsky points out, Khlestakov and Chichikov are pompous nonentities, false savior figures, satanic usurpers. The greatest usurper of them all, the Antichrist, had been cast in Vladimir Solovyov's turn-of-the-century prophecies as the real imminent threat to Russia. This eschatological vision left a deep imprint on Bely's early works. It was no coincidence that Sventsitsky, influenced as he was by Solovyov, should have made the Antichrist his hero in his partial self-revelation.

The usurper theme may be particularly viable in Russian culture. Russian history, after all, contains a series of self-appointed pretenders to the throne culminating in the false Dmitrys during the Time of Troubles. Significantly enough, two of Pushkin's most important works—the drama *Boris Godunov* and the short novel *The Captain's Daughter*—center on this theme. We also know that Rasputin's charlatanism would set its stamp on tsarist Russia in her death-throes. Bely seems more than anyone else to have intuited this. In his sketch published in the anthology *How We Write* (1933), he regrets not having combined *The Silver Dove* (begun immediately after Azef and Sventsitsky were exposed) and *Petersburg*, parts of a projected trilogy, into a single work in which the diabolical sectarian leader would operate near the court in the imperial capital: in such a case the prophecy about Rasputin would have been clearer. It is in a way built into the two novels nonetheless.

Sventsitsky's remaining life has a tragic-heroic dimension to it. In 1915 he published *Citizens of Heaven*, a book resulting from his journey to anchorite monks in the Caucasus. A few weeks before the October upheaval, he was ordained a priest. He is said to have retained much of his remarkable charisma, and his sermons attracted large crowds. In 1922-1925 he was exiled. Now once again he paradoxically began advocating a violent Christianity in the struggle with the Soviet state. Thus he did exactly the opposite of his erstwhile companion Brikhnichyov, who demonstrated a capacity for survival under Communist rule. Sventsitsky was arrested again in 1928 and died in a Siberian prison in 1931.

Oracle or Quack?

The memoirs of the Russian Symbolists abound in detailed physical portraits of Anna Mintslova. All of them mention her protruding eyes—"two rolling wheels," according to Andrey Bely—possessed of a penetrating hypnotic power. She concealed her considerable bulk behind what looked like a heavy shroud. She had a high forehead, a pronounced nose, and disheveled hair standing out in tufts. She often communicated with those around her in suggestive muffled whispers. Sometimes in a state of rapture her entire body would begin to shake. In the midst of all this, observers were struck not least by her beautiful hands and unusually long fingers. This woman—of almost indeterminate gender and, as described by Evgeniya Gertsyk in her memoirs, ageless—came to play a leading role in Symbolism's dramatic final stage. With the possible exception of Aleksandr Blok, she influenced all the major Symbolists, and without her we would not have Bely's two most important novels, *The Silver Dove* and *Petersburg*. Nor would we have Vyacheslav Ivanov's poetry collection *Cor ardens* or his late-Symbolist articles on theory, or many of Maksimilian Voloshin's major poems. Thus for several years this remarkable creature exerted a very strong and as yet not exhaustively studied influence on Russian literature. And then she mysteriously vanished. No one knows when, where, or under what circumstances she died.

A great deal can be said about Mintslova's background and how she came to be what she was. I venture to say that the key to her personality is to be found in her relationship to books. Her grandfather, Rudolf Mintslov Sr., was descended from German immigrants. A writer, archeologist, and bibliophile, he had been the curator of the Imperial Library in Petersburg. Her father, Rudolf Jr., was a lawyer by training, but he had also been active as a journalist and had made his home a liberal stronghold and meeting place for progressive writers, scientists and scholars, and politicians. The cult of the Book he established there embraced the natural sciences, and materialism and atheism in the spirit of the 1860s, and took the Enlightenment and French Revolution as its self-evident and constant points of reference. Like her younger brother Sergey, who became a prominent writer, archeologist, bibliographer, and bibliophile, Mintslova began browsing in the enormous family library at a very early age and soon became a voracious reader. As she once stated of her relationship to books: "I love books like living beings—they have souls, and even their fate thoroughly resembles our own: they as well are devoured by worms." What is remarkable, however, is that she early on chose to go a step further than her grandfather, father, and brother by infusing their radicalism with overtones of occultism. Books not only provided knowledge of material reality and called for changes in living conditions, but also awakened insights into a hidden spiritual world and the need to reshape physical reality itself. Books were like human beings, and human beings were like books. She seems to have learned to regard people and indeed the entire world—art, architecture, and nature—as an open book to be read and deciphered.

As has been observed elsewhere, the model with whom she increasingly identified was Helena Blavatsky, the mother of Theosophy. Blavatsky also had roots in the Russian intellectual milieu. Her mother, Elena Hahn, had been interested in women's issues and written tendentious novels in the early phase of Russian realism that had been praised by Vissarion Belinsky, the standard bearer of socially conscious literature. Helena Blavatsky had published a couple of poems in Russia around 1870. In 1875, in the United States, she founded the Theosophical Society. In *Isis Unveiled* and *The Secret Doctrine* she laid the foundation for her speculative attempt to bring together religions and various mystical creeds into a single whole. She has also been described as physically amorphous and hypnotically charismatic, and Mintslova obviously exploited these similarities. Directly echoing Blavatsky but on even flimsier grounds, she later claimed she was guided by Hindu mahatmas, and she even dressed like her predecessor and deliberately imitated her handwriting.

Mintslova enrolled in Blavatsky's Theosophical movement around the turn of the century. She was constantly not only reading but also traveling, yet another feature that links her to Blavatsky. She participated in international Theosophical congresses and became personally acquainted with the leading figures of the movement, especially Annie Besant, who had a radical political background in the Fabian Society. These contacts were made easier by the fact that she—like Blavatsky—spoke several European languages. Mintslova soon established a personal relationship with Rudolf Steiner, the leader of the German section of the Theosophical Society. She came to regard herself as Steiner's special emissary to Russia, and she was also his first Russian translator. Despite her French upbringing, she gradually turned more and more toward Germany, and she was the first to introduce Novalis to Russia.

Bely met Mintslova while still a child in the 1880s. His earliest memory of her was connected with books. He recalls in his memoirs that as a young girl she was given the task of organizing Vladimir Taneev's large library in Demyanovo near Moscow. A lawyer and the composer Sergey's brother, Taneev was a member of Mintslova's father's intimate circle of freethinkers. In the 1890s she became acquainted with poets such as Maksimilian Voloshin, Konstantin Balmont, and Valery Bryusov. The latter notes in his diaries that he held her insights into lyrical poetry in high regard. She was already adept at interpreting texts and at deciphering people. It was a happy combination of talents, for she had acquired the singular ability to elevate others by bringing out their flattering subtexts, their underutilized talents and dormant genius. Bely glimpsed her in various literary contexts early in the century, but he kept his distance. He had read Blavatsky already as a teenager, but at the time he was most interested in Vladimir Solovyov, Nietzsche, and Ibsen.

Mintslova's real entrance into Symbolist circles dates from the revolutionary year 1905, when she came into closer contact with the poet Maksimilian Voloshin in France. She travelled with

Anna Mintslova, 1905.

him and his artist companion Margarita Sabashnikova, whom she persuaded him to marry. For Voloshin, who also was a painter, acquaintance with Mintslova proved stimulating. She analyzed works of art—not least in the Louvre—and architecture such as the Gothic cathedrals in Rouen and Chartres. He responded with a suite of poems on the Rouen Cathedral that was entirely under her influence. The seven sections of the suite reflect her description of the seven esoteric steps in life that seemed to be expressed symbolically in the medieval building. The French Revolution acquired a new dimension for him when she pointed out its esoteric undercurrents. Most important of all, perhaps, was that she explained who he really was and the great tasks that awaited him.

Through Voloshin, Mintslova became acquainted with another Symbolist, Vyacheslav Ivanov, and was soon a frequent guest in his "Tower" in Petersburg. When, in the fall of 1906, Ivanov and his wife and colleague Lidiya Zinovyeva-Annibal tried a bisexual experiment in cohabitation with Sabashnikova and the poet Sergey Gorodetsky, Mintslova was involved as a commentator on the various spiritual needs of the contracting parties, and also as support for Voloshin in his acute matrimonial difficulties. Other inhabitants and guests of the Tower also came under her influence—Mikhail Kuzmin, for example, who wrote a number of poems based on the occult meditation exercises to which she had introduced him.

When Zinovyeva-Annibal died in the fall of 1907, Mintslova became Ivanov's even closer confidante. Soon she moved into the Tower. The mourning Ivanov hoped she could help him establish contact with his deceased wife. Observing all this from the side, and herself in love with Ivanov, Evgeniya Gertsyk noted in her memoirs that like an invisible "bat," Mintslova possessed an unrivalled ability to worm herself in anywhere there was tragedy and misery.

Now she mustered all her manipulative talents. She elevated Ivanov's poetry to the level of almost divine clairvoyance, praising it as a brilliant array of symbols without equal in Russia. In her interpretation the most trivial everyday details assumed cosmic significance. Everything surrounding Ivanov and Mintslova seemed to be signs pregnant with meaning. She guided him through the various stages of esoteric initiation, leaving her mark on his theory of symbols as she did so. At the same time, she injected unmistakeable erotic overtones into their contacts. Several poems in Ivanov's collection *Cor ardens* had their origin in impressions from this intense interaction. The very title suggests the parity she declared to exist between physical microcosm and planetary macrocosm, between the heart and the sun.

In the fall of 1908 something happened. Mintslova entered a new phase and became indispensable not only to Ivanov but also to Bely, with whom Ivanov was becoming more involved. Suddenly what she had to offer answered the needs of the Symbolist movement, for in its incipient crisis it looked more and more to both occultism and nationalism. Little by little, Mintslova began to rebel against the secretary of the important German section of the International Theosophical society Rudolf Steiner and to regard herself as his equal. Very much in keeping with the somewhat paranoid spirit of the time in the wake of the abortive 1905 Revolution, she expressed herself in nationalistic and increasingly downright reactionary terms. For example, when Bely had a hysterical fit at an innocuous literary soirée in early 1909 and began pointing out "enemies" around him, Mintslova was there to confirm his projections. She subsequently initiated him into her Steinerian meditation program, which served as an important source for Bely's first novel *The Silver Dove*, which he worked on throughout 1909. The plot revolves around the satanic anti-Russian machinations of a flagellant sect that snares the Symbolist poet and spiritual visionary Daryalsky in its toils and has him murdered just as he is about to escape.

As early as the fall of 1908 Mintslova had taken note of Bely's anti-Semitic article "Stamped Culture," which he had written under the influence of his friend and mentor, the increasingly militant racist Emilii Medtner. By this time her arguments were openly anti-Semitic, and she had also begun referring to Vladimir Solovyov's warnings about "Panmongolism," by which was meant the aggressive expansion of the "yellow race." More and more forcefully, she impressed upon Ivanov and Bely the idea that only Symbolism could save the nation at this fateful moment in history. Comparing them to medieval Russia's princes, she declared that they, as the leaders of the movement, were summoned to combat covert infiltration from the East. They must put aside their earlier conflicts and unite as "the feudal princes of culture." Her argument speaks eloquently of her belief in the power of literature, for it envisions nothing less than a cosmic battle in which Holy Russia is called upon to defend the Aryan world on the cultural frontier.

It is interesting to note that the Musagetes (Musaget) publishing house that Emilii Medtner built up with the support of Bely, Ellis and Ivanov in 1909 to unite the fractured Symbolist movement soon came to regard itself to some extent as the esoteric cultural bulwark Mintslova was advocating. Everyone in the Musagetes circle was at one time or another under her hypnotic influence—including Medtner, who, despite his pronounced hostility to occultism, was vulnerable to her pronouncements on his own extremely responsible mission.

So where were these enemies that were already on their way to conquer Russia? They had already secured a foothold in both Moscow and Petersburg. Mintslova referred to them in letters and other statements as an obscurely italicized "they." They were said to be satanic Oriental occultists and sectarians, secretly pursuing their destructive purposes in intimate collaboration with the Jews. Their agenda included human sacrifice and ritual murder, various forms of bestial violence, poisoning, and spraying the air with toxic fluids. Mintslova claimed that she had received death threats, and that her enemies resorted to lies, insanity, obsession, hypnosis, and magic. One important base of operations was in Helsingfors (Helsinki), where they were supposedly practicing ancient Finnish sorcery. Mintslova was evidently sensitive to changes in the overall atmosphere, for soon, in 1911, all of Russia would be seized by a wave—albeit clearly orchestrated from above—of national paranoia. Mendel Beilis, an innocent Jewish bookkeeper in Kiev, was tried for a ritual murder, while the falsified *Protocols of the Elders of Zion* and pamphlets insinuating a Jewish conspiracy—many of them with occult undertones—were widely disseminated throughout the country.

What is remarkable is that almost all of Mintslova's warnings could be applied to her as well. After all, with her extensive background in Buddhism, she herself was surely an "Oriental occultist." She claimed to be in continuous contact with higher spiritual Rosicrucian beings who gave her instructions, and this mysterious brotherhood was in fact no less diffuse a *"they"* than her enemies. It was moreover obvious to the critical eye—and all of her followers had secret reservations about her—that she as well resorted to hypnosis and magic, and perhaps ultimately to lies, deceit, and fraud. She visited Finland often, sending vivid reports from Helsingfors, the city she especially associated with dangerous sorcery. She expatiated about the demonic Easterners' "raving" and "insanity," but what did she herself preach? One word and its derivatives of which she was especially fond was "madness," which for her generally carried positive connotations. Everything about her was suggestively double-edged. Was she herself perhaps precisely what she was so forcefully warning against?

Eventually, both Ivanov and Bely began to question her authority. In the Tower, Mikhail Kuzmin was already beginning to poke fun at her in his prose writings. Ivanov's and Bely's reservations originated from a latent rivalry between the two men. Mintslova argued that Bely was part of a mystical triangle at the top of the Russian cultural defense, where he was complemented by an as yet unnamed spiritual leader. Bely gradually realized that this "other" person was quite simply Ivanov, and that Moscow and the Musagetes collective were thus being put into the same category as Petersburg. Mintslova, moreover, seemed to be giving Ivanov priority, for although in Bely's eyes he was a novice in occultism who was just flirting with his newly acquired knowledge, he was presented as Steiner's superior and successor. At the same time, both Bely and Ivanov increasingly felt that Mintslova's spiritual brotherhood was not entirely credible. Promised contacts failed to materialize.

Things were getting too hot for Mintslova, and she began talking more and more vaguely about needing to leave everything and get away. She had not accomplished her mission and must therefore take her punishment. This, of course, was a new strategy designed to make those around her feel guilty. Sometimes, her imminent departure implied immersion in a life of monastic asceticism, while at others it meant nothing less than a farewell to life itself. Early on, Bely had dreamed of breaking free in various ways from the humdrum of life and urban culture, perhaps to take up a monastic life, perhaps to seek the communion he so desired with the religious spirit of the people. This is a recurrent motif in his works. Mintslova was of course aware of this background, and it was Bely in particular whom she sought to influence with her talk of an inevitable farewell. In late August 1910, she disappeared just as she had predicted. Some claimed she had entered a Jesuit monastery in Italy, while others believed that she really had crossed the ultimate boundary and voluntarily gone to her death.

In November 1910, at the Religious and Philosophical Society in Moscow, Bely held a lecture on Tolstoy and Dostoevsky and the "tragedy of creation." Evidently to some extent influenced by Mintslova's disappearance, the theme of parting was central. Like a true Russian pilgrim in search of a higher truth that he may have hoped to find in the disciplined life of a monastery, Tolstoy had fled Yasnaya Polyana just a few days before. In the introduction to his lecture, Bely interpreted his sudden departure as a step beyond Dostoevsky, a religious act fraught with enormous apocalyptic consequences for Russia, an event that leads him to recall the medieval struggle against the Tartars.

Bely himself broke away only a month later when he set off on a long trip abroad accompanied by Asya Turgeneva. When they returned in the spring of 1911 they both immersed themselves in the study of Theosophy. Bely began planning the publication of *Trudy i dni* (*Works and Days*), a Musagetes journal to be edited by Bely, Ivanov, and Blok, which to some extent was to follow Mintslova's exhortations to defend Symbolism and the national idea. Their planned collaboration was soon cut short, however. Blok and Ivanov withdrew, as did Bely not long after, when his adherence to Steiner became a reality and his differences with Medtner intensified.

Soon Bely began working on *Petersburg*, which to an even greater degree than its predecessor came to be colored by Mintslova's phobias. In that novel, the diabolical Orient has taken over the Russian capital, and the terrorist leader Lippanchenko has clearly Mongol physical features. All dimensions are interwoven in the fabric of the novel, and all proportions seem to be inverted. This of course is an application of Gogol's artistic method, where the significant and the trivial constantly exchange places, but it also echoes Mintslova's worldview, in which a trifle could be elevated to a cosmic drama.

The fall of 1911 Voloshin spent in Paris, where he wrote a memorial poem for Mintslova, who by this time definitely seemed to be gone:

> Burning above her was
> A crown of madness and fire.
> And the flame of torture,
> And her clairvoyant hands,
> And the unseeing lead of her eyes,
> Her face of a Gothic Sybil,
> And the heaviness of her lids and harshness of her cheeks,
> The uneven gait of her steps—
> All was full of oracular power.
> Her rambling speech,
> Shimmering with nocturnal light,
> Sounded like a summons and a response.
> A mysterious blueness
> Marked her out among the living...
> And hopefully to her I ran
> From the primeval dreams of being
> Encircling me from all around.

Soon Bely made a new and even more radical break with the past. In the spring of 1912 he and Turgeneva travelled west and settled first in Brussels, where they met with a series of occult experiences that included visions and auditory and olfactory sensations. It was as though the "other side" was attempting to communicate with

Andrey Bely, 1922.

them, as though they had entered a Mintslovian world of signs and cryptic signals. The pair ended up with Rudolf Steiner in Cologne and later joined his Theosophical Commune in Munich. This step proved to be extremely fruitful for the novel, which also plays on the ambiguity in Mintslova's preaching and doomsday prophecies rooted in the esoteric meditation into which she had originally initiated Bely.

Significantly enough, in the various versions of his memoirs Bely continued to grapple with Mintslova. The detailed portrait he paints of her in 1922 in the as yet unpublished drafts of the reminiscences he wrote in Berlin is still ambivalent throughout. He declares that in her presence earthly laws no longer applied, that she was a planet in her own right, a constellation all her own: "the boundaries between 'madness' and 'common sense,' between 'up' and 'down' disappeared tumultuously into a cosmos of different dimensions." He goes on to add: "to this day I throw up my hands before the question: what was *'all this'*: madness, a fantasy, delirium, clairvoyance, lies, or everything together?" He emphasizes in conclusion: "What she was in her true aspect—mentally ill, a degenerate, a fraud, a dreamer, an oracle, a flagellant, a criminal—this will remain a secret to us."

In *Between Two Revolutions*, the third volume of his memoirs published just over a decade later in Stalin's Soviet Union, Bely is prepared to dismiss her once and for all, which may to some extent be due to circumstances. He subjects her to devastating satire: she was a bloated "occult cow," a fleshy lump bumping along in a sack whose voice seemed to come from her belly; in the final analysis she was merely a Russian Peer Gynt, a deranged charlatan. It deserves to be noted that Bely here explicitly disdains her "delirium" as "abracadabra," the same word the young terrorists in *Petersburg* use when speaking about their inner demons.

What is curious is that this "occult cow," this grotesque creature in a sack, was able to help Bely accomplish such great artistic deeds and make such crucial decisions. Out of his meeting with Rudolf Steiner and what would soon be known as Anthroposophy came an unequalled work of prose. Russian literature quite definitely owes a considerable debt of gratitude to Anna Mintslova.

Janko Lavrin—
Pan-Slavist Across the Spectrum

Janko Lavrin was born in 1887 in Krupa, a Slovenian village of fewer than ten houses in Bela Krajina. A subject of the Habsburg Empire, upon completing the Gymnasium in 1907 he "fled" to Russia to avoid military service. More importantly, however, he was inspired by the new Pan-Slavic ideas that had taken shape around the turn of the century—dreams of liberation from the Viennese yoke and the creation of a Slavic cultural community. This was a radical Pan-Slavism, not a variant of the grandiose old Russian dream of Slavic subjects led by a tsarist power.

Thus it was Russia to which Lavrin now turned, with the nationalist Dostoevsky as his spiritual guide. There was a paradox here. Lavrin dreamed of becoming a writer himself, and he had been strongly influenced by patriotic young Slovenian poets. Besides the dream of a Christian Slavic community, what the young Slovene found appealing in the great Russian artist was Dostoevsky's liberating vision of society and humanity. Full of hatred for the Habsburg overlords and contemptuous of the German language, he wanted to help erect a Slavic bulwark against the Empire.

In Petersburg he soon came into contact with people of a like mind. He began studying linguistics and archeology at the university, but not much came of it. In 1908, a Pan-Slavist Congress convened in Prague drafted a "Neo-Slavic" program. Lavrin soon made the acquaintance of influential figures who became rather like mentors to the early-orphaned 20-year-old. The deepest impression was made by the erudite Czech philosopher and politician Tomáš Masaryk, who shared his interest in Russian spirituality, Dostoevsky, Tolstoy, and various manifestations of Slavophilism. Lavrin was already entertaining advanced plans of founding an all-Slavic cultural periodical published in Russian. It would be called *Slavyansky mir* (*The Slavic World*).

At this point, just as the first issue of the journal was about to appear, on October 6, 1908, Austria annexed Bosnia and Herzegovina. The attack, of course, gave fresh fuel to Pan-Slavic ideas. Suddenly previously rather indifferent Russian intellectuals were awakened to the cause of their oppressed South Slavic brethren cultures. Two months later, Tolstoy himself launched a vehement protest against what had happened. At this opportune moment, *Slavyansky mir* published its first issue, much of it written by Lavrin himself under various pseudonyms. Aspiring to become a Russian debater and writer, as editor he called himself Ivan Lavrin. He explained in an anonymous editorial that without claiming any superiority, Russian was well suited to be the Slavs' lingua franca. The goal was to use the Russian language to harness the great contemporary literatures of the various fraternal countries to the common cause.

Janko Lavrin portrayed by Boris Kustodiev, 1909.

Not much later, in 1909, another issue appeared. Eventually Lavrin was in fact busy translating from five different languages: Slovenian, Polish, Czech, Slovakian, and Belarusian. In the summer of that year another Pan-Slavic Congress was held in Petersburg. Lavrin's responsible position of secretary allowed him to establish important new connections. Masaryk considered it almost his mission to win over Tolstoy to the movement. In April 1910, he visited the writer at Yasnaya Polyana, from where he wrote a letter to Lavrin that concluded: "Lev Nikolaevich sends you his greetings." That meant that Tolstoy had been informed about Lavrin's activities, was familiar with *Slavyansky mir,* and supported the cause. As soon became apparent from Lavrin's obituary of Tolstoy in the journal, however, his feelings for the writer were not unambiguous. He admired Tolstoy as an artist, but despite his own religious interests he did not understand his preaching. As he explained to me when I met him in London 76 years later, what he wanted was to move forward toward a better world, not back to a pre-civilized state in which we lived by the work of our hands in village collectives.

In the summer of 1910, the next Pan-Slavic Congress was held in Sofia. Soon an all-Slavic union of academics and writers was founded with Lavrin as secretary that had as its express purpose to promote collaboration among Slavs engaged in scholarly and literary activities. Half of Lavrin's life was in literature, and his world outlook and view of humanity were shaped not least by Dostoevsky. This gave him a special kinship with the Russian Symbolists, whose views were rooted in Dostoevsky and influenced in particular by the prophetic dimension of his novels and the mixed mood of anticipation and anguish that marked the age. In 1911, *Slavyansky mir* ceased publication. The final issue contained a very important editorial in which Lavrin took exception to the current of nineteenth-century Pan-Slavism that focused exclusively on Russian imperial ambitions. In conformity with the spirit of the time, however, he did believe in a Slavic "race."

Instead of *Slavyansky mir*, Lavrin and the Petersburg Symbolist Sergey Gorodetsky began planning a Slavic literary almanac. It was called *Veles*, after the South Slavic pagan god who was the protector of the arts. On its pages, the Russian Symbolists would publish alongside contemporary Slavic colleagues of similar orientation. At the same time, however, Symbolism was in a deep crisis and about to be succeeded by rebellious young Futurists, who reacted against sacerdotal poses and mystical ambitions by speaking the language of the street and experimenting with fractured grammar and syntax. Lavrin was soon at home among them as well. In late evenings at the Brodyachaya sobaka (The Stray Dog) literary cabaret in Petersburg, he would meet them and observe their antics.

Lavrin's interests included hiking in the mountains. In the summer of 1912 he and his Petersburg friend Mikhail Le Dantue traveled down to the Caucasus, where they visited the brothers Ilya and Kirill Zdanevich, who had grown up in Tbilisi. Kirill was a member of the so called Rayonnists, an artistic group led by Mikhail Larionov and his wife Natalya Goncharova. In the spring of that year he had become interested in the nativist paintings of the destitute Georgian artist Niko Pirosmani. The young avant-gardists were at the time attracted to so-called primitive art, not least for the kind of signboards that Pirosmani painted for taverns and wine cellars, often as payment for his drinking bouts. Le Dantue and the Zdanevich brothers began systematically collecting his remaining paintings, and now in 1912 the undertaking was continued by Lavrin and Le Dantue. Soon Pirosmani was being exhibited alongside Kazimir Malevich and Marc Chagall. Today he is a Georgian national treasure with his own museum in Tbilisi.

The constant traveler Lavrin did more than this, however. That year he also attended the Pan-Slavic Congress in Prague, hosted by Masaryk. Secretly (since he was a deserter), he visited Ljubljana and came into closer contact with Preporod (Rebirth), a group of young writers whose program included the establishment of a specifically South Slavic national community. He was aware that the entire region was in ferment. In October 1912 the so called First Balkan War broke out, followed by another in February 1913.

It was at this point that Lavrin met Velimir Khlebnikov in the company of Vladimir Mayakovsky, then a mere teenager. Lavrin must have appeared at just the right moment in Khlebnikov's life. Although known as a Futurist, Khlebnikov was more at home in the past. Dreaming of resurrecting a Slavic proto-language, for several years he had been steeping himself in South Slavic myths and folklore. His growing interest had focused especially on the Montenegro nation and their heroic history and profusion of living myths. He had been planning to travel there since 1909, and now suddenly these dreams were given new life by the little mountain people's brave rebellion against the Turks that sparked the Balkan War.

Lavrin soon moved the homeless poet into his Petersburg apartment, where Khlebnikov had an opportunity to browse Lavrin's extensive South Slavic library, upon which he drew for his poetic experiments. He was a verbal magician who believed in a special bond between word and deed, and it occurred to him that the expressive Montenegrin language, spoken by a people that throughout five centuries had successfully defended its freedom and ancient customs, possessed intimate ties with proto-Slavic. As Lavrin told me in our 1986 conversation, Khlebnikov would sometimes almost go into ecstasy over a single colorful Montenegrin word.

The first issue of *Veles* now conveniently appeared, full of texts by Andrey Bely and other Symbolists. "Petrograd" rather than "Petersburg" was indicated as the place of publication, almost as though Lavrin had managed to be influenced by Khlebnikov's efforts to resurrect Church Slavic. Two years later, wartime patriotism would in fact rename the city.

Soon, Lavrin got an offer from the conservative newspaper *Novoe vremya* (*New Time*) to become its international reporter at large. He seemed to be at home everywhere. The assignment provided him with stable finances and fantastic opportunities to travel throughout Europe. In June 1913, when Bely was in the middle of his work on *Petersburg*, Lavrin showed up at the writer's side in Helsingfors and attended Rudolf Steiner's lectures on the future of Europe and Russia's national soul. For a little while he became an adherent of the new "spiritual science."

Lavrin's position at this time was utterly unique. On the one hand he was employed by the ultraconservative *Novoe vremya*, but on the other he was an ally of the most radical literary and artistic subversives. In the middle of it all, he was attracted to Steiner's occult doctrines. He moved freely through Europe. News of the shot in Sarajevo found him hiking in the Pyrenees. A month later the war broke out. It came as no surprise to him, for he had long known that the explosion in the Balkans was imminent. A bit later, in early 1915, he and Sergey Gorodetsky published another all-Slavic volume, called *Perun* after the Slavic god of thunder. Here, albeit somewhat more modestly this time, South Slavs and Russians were together again.

Lavrin knew how to distinguish between his own interests and friendships. Admitting the Futurist rebels into the pages of these Pan-Slavic publications was out of the question, although Khlebnikov perhaps might have fit in. The Zdanevich brothers and Le Dantue were pushing their extreme positions even further than before, founding a group called "The Bloodless Murder," in whose name during the war years they published ten handwritten or hectographed little magazines—great rarities today—in which they proclaimed the "aesthetics of the insignificant" and indulged in a peculiar avant-garde self-irony, a kind of playful absurdism.

In the fall of 1915 *Novoe vremya* decided to dispatch Lavrin to the Balkans as a war correspondent. In Montenegro he had an audience with King Nikola; in Albania he was granted an interview with the self-appointed ruler Essad Pasha. In the tent of an officer in Serbia he met a peculiar figure in a worn guerilla uniform who wanted to share with him his nightly dreams. It was Milan Ciganović, the man who handed the pistol to Gavrilo Princip in Sarajevo. Lavrin drew on these experiences for a book published in the fall of 1916: *In the Land of Eternal War*, subtitled *Albanian Sketches*. Toward the end of that year he came back to to Russia to supervise publication.

By that time the gap between the decorated war correspondent and the anti-aesthete of "The Bloodless Murder" had become too wide. Lavrin's roles were no longer compatible. In a hectographed issue of the magazine, Le Dantue and the artist Olga Leshkova lampooned his dramatic war experiences in hilarious captioned drawings. Ilya Zdanevich followed up the satiric attack with an absurd opera featuring "Janko" in the lead role. His "dra," as he referred to his transrational dramatic works, was entitled *Janko krUl albAnskaj* (approximately, *Janko kUng of the albAnyuns*). Written in the transrational language launched by Khlebnikov and Kruchonykh, it had its premiere in an artist's studio in Petrograd around the turn of the year 1916-1917. In the simple plot, an "Albanian" gang of bandits decides to force the terrified Janko to ascend the kingdom's vacant throne. It is prophetic to the degree that it describes a regime change three months before the February Revolution. Janko tries to get off the throne, so to be on the safe side the bandits glue him to it. With the help of a German doctor he tries to tear himself loose, but he is discovered by the bandits and is ultimately shot.

Following another visit to the Balkans, Lavrin was evacuated together with Serbian soldiers from the front in the fall of 1917, ending up in London. Then came the news of the Bolshevik coup in Russia. He realized that perhaps for a long time he would not be able to return to what had become his second homeland, and he began intensively studying English. He "learned" the language by writing a study of Dostoevsky's historical significance based on his own experiences with the Symbolists that in the late winter of 1918 was published in several issues of the avant-garde journal *The New Age*. The work was specially commissioned by Lavrin's new friend editor-in-chief Alfred Richard Orage, who was interested in psychoanalysis, radical social theories, and occultism (which soon would lead him to Gurdjieff's "school of consciousness" outside Paris). Two years later, Lavrin's *Dostoevsky: A Psycho-critical Study* appeared in book form.

The cover of Janko Lavrin's **In the Land of Eternal War**, *Petrograd 1916.*

It seemed now that the Pan-Slavic project had come to an end in war and revolution. The Habsburg Empire was overthrown, and soon Yugoslavia and Czechoslovakia would emerge as independent states (the latter with Tomáš Masaryk, Lavrin's friend, as president). Lavrin decided on a third writing career in his third language. Soon, he was offered a newly established professorship in Nottingham, and he chose to become a scholar.

The "Swede" in the Late Nineteenth- and Early Twentieth-Century Russian Culture— and His Daughter

On February 28, 1909, Aleksey Venkstern died in Moscow at the age of 52. No cause of death was indicated—he may have committed suicide.

Venkstern's family was of German-Swedish extraction. Let us take a look at how it came to Russia.

The battle of Lesnaya between Swedish and Russian armies in what is today Belarus took place on September 29, 1708. Although the clash itself was a stalemate, the Swedish withdrawal was so undisciplined and poorly organized that it was tantamount to a defeat, and many Swedes fell behind and were taken prisoner. The loss, in fact, laid the groundwork for Charles XII's historic defeat at Poltava in 1709.

A number of Swedish officers reported missing in action had in reality ended up in captivity. One of them was Jacob Wenckstern, whom the Swedes reported as killed. In reality he soon switched sides, and he was such an able soldier that he came to the attention of Peter the Great himself.

Jacob Wenckstern was the son of Christoffer Wenckstern, who had as a very young man immigrated to Stockholm in 1631 from Germany and made himself a name as a talented and highly skilled bookbinder. Born in 1659, Jacob—the future Yakov Venkstern— was the eldest of nine children, only three of whom survived.

In Russia, Yakov married late in life and had a son named Khristofor, who also became an army officer and in turn fathered

Aleksey Venkstern and his wife Olga a few years before his death.

another Yakov, who made a career in the civil service and attained the rank of Court Counselor. Yakov Jr. married a sister of the philosopher Pyotr Chaadaev and fathered ten children. One of his sons studied together with Mikhail Lermontov, while another, Aleksey, rose to the ranking of gubernial secretary. In the late nineteenth century, his daughter Aleksandra Venkstern became well known as the author of a series of novels with melodramatic plots revolving around love, suicide, and disease, and scored a praise of Lev Tolstoy. Her brother Aleksey was born in 1852, the great-great-great-grandson of the Stockholm bookbinder, and he died in 1909. In an obituary of him, Sergey Solovyov noted that, with his light blue eyes and long white beard, Aleksey Venkstern Jr. looked like a Viking. The soul within, however, was more Russian than Swedish. He spent his entire life as an affluent landowner on his family estate, Laptevo, on the border of the Moscow and Tula provinces, but at the time of his death he had been forced to sell his property and was bankrupt.

Those who knew Aleksey Venkstern emphasize his sensual appetite for life and his uniquely broad artistic talent. At the same time, he suffered from manic depression and regularly occurring mood swings. The political resignation that set in after the newly awakened hopes of 1905 in Russian society seems to have interacted with his own unsuccessful financial speculations and his descent into serious depression. In an attempt to escape it Venkstern devoted himself to his hobbies. He led a free and irresponsible life filled with hunting, dog breeding, extravagant parties and wild troika rides. He cultivated all sorts of artistic interests and tried to adopt a kind of artistic lifestyle. Venkstern wrote poems, many of them light pastiches, in the spirit of Pushkin. Published only in periodicals and never

The "Swede" in Russian Culture—and His Daughter

Double cousins Natalya Venkstern and Sofya Giatsintova, undated.

brought out as a book, they were highly regarded among his acquaintances. In the 1870s and 1880s he had belonged to a legendary amateur Shakespeare society, led by pedagogue and pushkinist Lev Polivanov, which put on plays of considerable aesthetic worth. He himself often took the lead roles, giving superb performances as Hamlet, Coriolanus, Henry V, and others. Ivan Turgenev, for one, was occasionally in attendance. Sometimes Aleksey Venkstern, often in collaboration with his brother-in-law, the art historian Vladimir Giatsintov, would himself write plays for the group. His Hamlet is said to be among the best ever seen on the Russian stage. We can surmise that the Danish prince's existential desperation and vacillation on the brink of suicide were themes particularly close to Venkstern's frame of mind.

Being also strongly attracted to Spanish culture, Venkstern had early on traveled to Spain and translated Agustín Moreto y Cabaña's sparklingly witty seventeenth-century comedy *Spite for Spite* into Russian. A telling choice, the plot centers on a proud, highly accomplished seducer's conquest of an equally proud woman. Venkstern had many affairs that often ended in scandal, but he survived them all and was forgiven by his wife, a Giatsintov whose inherited family traits of patience and a calm sense of duty were the exact opposite of his own.

Aleksey Venkstern's sudden death caused his sixteen-year-old daughter Natalya, who was very devoted to him, to fall seriously ill in the fall of 1909. Her contact with reality was thoroughly and gravely disturbed. She experienced strange somnambulistic states, hallucinations and cramps, and suicidal moods. At times she found it difficult to recognize her own relatives. She was placed in the care of the prominent neurologist Vladimir Rot at the Moscow University Nerve Clinic where she met one of Rot's younger colleagues,

Aleksandr Vyakhirev, who was interested in the new Freudian therapy that had just been introduced in Russia and decided to try it on her.

Her friend Sergey Solovyov, who after his own father's premature death had come to regard Venkstern as a surrogate father and found a new home in the free bohemian atmosphere of his estate, himself fell ill a short while later. What brought it on was an unhappy love affair with Natalya's "double cousin"—or as she herself called her, her "sister"—Sofya Giatsintova.

How had Natalya's father come to play so central a role in her life that his death gave rise to such serious emotional problems? Father and daughter had been very close to each other, and were said to be much alike both outwardly and inwardly. She had a sister and two brothers, but she was his favorite. Shaped early on by this frivolous artistic milieu, she had inherited his talents and wanted to follow in his footsteps and become an actress.

After completing her first round of therapy with Rot and Vyakhirev, Natalya and her cousin both applied to work under Konstantin Stanislavsky at the Moscow Art Theater. Giatsintova, who was also a Venkstern, but on her mother's side, was admitted and began a promising stage career, but Natalya was not accepted. This failure contributed to the need for more therapy sessions in 1910-1912. An important component of her clinical picture now was her overwrought fixation on Vasily Kachalov, the Art Theater's (and Russia's) leading character actor, who became the new venerated father figure in her life.

In the spring of 1911, a number of professors and lecturers, including Rot and Vyakhirev, left Moscow University to protest the growing political repression. Together with a colleague, in January 1912 Vyakhirev developed the Podsolnechnoye clinic near Moscow into a full-time sanatorium. Natalya Venkstern continued her treatment there at the same time that Sergey Solovyov began psychoanalytical therapy at the nearby Kryukovo sanatorium. This was deep psychology's year in Russia.

Vyakhirev had just published a Russian translation of Freud's *Three Essays on the Theory of Sexuality*. His intensive therapy appears to have succeeded in strengthening Natalya and freeing her from her fixation on Kachalov. Healing may have come at a high and dangerous price, however, for precisely like Sabina Spielrein, the Russian psychoanalytical patient whom Jung treated at the Burghölzli Clinic in Zurich, she fell in love with her savior, and her feelings were reciprocated. In the midst of all this, Vyakhirev died suddenly of appendicitis in the late summer of 1912 while visiting the Venkstern summer home outside Moscow. He had been considered an outstandingly talented therapist. His demise was a hard blow not only for Natalya but for Russian psychiatry as well. Things went better for Sergey Solovyov, who was declared cured and got married.

Aleksandr Vyakhirev, undated.

In its second issue of 1914, a few months before the outbreak of WWI, *Psikhoterapiya* (*Psychotherapy*), the leading organ for Russian deep psychology, carried an article by Dr. Mikhail Asatiani, Vyakhirev's colleague at Podsolnechnoye. It documented a detailed account of a case of feminine "hysteria" characterized by somnambulism, temporary loss of contact with reality, cramps, and suicidal moods that he claimed he and Vyakhirev had successfully treated. It is difficult to imagine that the woman in question could be anyone but Natalya Venkstern. The patient was said to have undergone successive rounds of therapy between 1909 and 1912 at the Moscow University Nerve Clinic and at Podsolnechnoye. She had a rich imagination and strong literary interests. She was the daughter of a manic depressive (born the same year as Aleksey Venkstern) and grew up on a country estate. She was reported to have two brothers and two sisters, which is correct if we take into account Giatsintova's declaration that from Natalya's early childhood, she was like a sister to her. Asatiani's share of the treatment, which included extensive Jungian association tests, is described in detail.

The tests indicated an "inversion syndrome," a sexual infirmity related to what Freud describes in *Three Essays*, the very work Vyakhirev had translated.

Natalya Venkstern recovered enough to be able to work and, following in her father's footsteps here as well, began an entirely new career as a writer. In commemoration of the centennial of the Decembrist uprising, her play *1825* was staged in the fall of 1925 on experimental stage No. 2 at the Moscow Art Theater parallel to and in a close interplay with Bely's new dramatized version of *Petersburg*. Both plays were directed by Mikhail Chekhov (Anton's nephew), himself influenced by both psychoanalysis and Anthroposophy, and Sofya in *Petersburg* was played by none other than Sofya Giatsintova.

Mikhail Bulgakov as the judge in *The Pickwick Papers*, 1934.

While Sofya Giatsintova soon became a celebrated theatre and film actress with a broad repertoire of roles ranging from Ibsen's Nora to Lenin's mother, Natalya made a name for herself in Soviet literature and was very productive despite recurrent psychic problems and an unstable private life. She wrote mostly for the younger generation, but she also became known for her stage adaptations of Dickens's novels. At the Moscow Art Theater she began collaboration—and a long and complex romantic relationship—with a new father figure in her life, Mikhail Bulgakov. It was he who helped her polish the lines of her successful dramatization of *The Posthumous Papers of the Pickwick Club*, which opened in 1934. Bulgakov himself took part in the play, thereby fulfilling the role of paternal surrogate in a dual sense, as both author and actor. *The Pickwick Club* was followed 15 years later by *Dombey and Son*. Some of her adaptations are said to have been adopted by British theaters.

Natalya and her psychoanalytical experience may have been of assistance to Bulgakov when he himself suffered from psychic problems in the politically tense situation of the 1930s. It was not without reason that his alter ego in his emerging novel *The Master and Margarita* takes refuge in a mental clinic. It is known that Bulgakov, himself a physician, was interested in psychodynamic therapies.

Sofya Giatsintova had a successful career in Soviet theater that culminated in a Stalin Prize. Natalya remained the same restless spirit as ever up until her death in 1957. As Giatsintova sums her up in her memoirs: "I have never met such a combination of charming, multifaceted talent and deep disharmony."

Blok and Strindberg's Face

Except for the last months, when he had ceased writing and became mentally ill, 1911-1912 was the darkest period in Aleksandr Blok's life. The Russian Symbolist movement had disintegrated. All that remained was desperation and the faintly dawning hope that someday the contours of a new Russia would somehow emerge.

During this somber time, August Strindberg gradually became vitally important to Blok. He was especially interested in Strindberg's face, in which he thought he detected features of the "new man" of the future and found spiritual strength and healing. Strindberg the man and Strindberg the writer were in Blok's eyes inseparable, and it was especially the autobiographical works that aroused his interest.

Strindberg had been brought to the attention of Blok's friend and colleague Vladimir Pyast (Pestovsky) by Anna Vrubel, the sister of the recently deceased painter Mikhail Vrubel. In the fall of 1910 she gave Pyast a copy of Strindberg's novel *Alone*, which Pyast soon passed on to Blok. The melancholic meditative prose of the work seemed to speak directly to both Pyast and Blok, describing their own experiences in their own language. Blok immediately sensed in Strindberg a kinsman and predecessor who had been tempered through suffering. The very title of the novel seemed to summarize Blok's predicament. He increasingly isolated himself from his fellow writers and artists in Petersburg and surrounded himself with just a few close friends, among them Pyast, to whom he became closely bound, particularly in the latter's capacity as a "guide" to Strindberg. Blok looked upon him as a Westerner and a link to West European culture, and it is on that basis that he perceived a connection between him and Strindberg.

In February 1911, Blok read *The Red Room*. At the same time, on Blok's suggestion, Pyast began reading Flaubert's *Sentimental Education*, one of Blok's favorite novels. Its portrayal of how a young man is molded into a demonic individualist unfit for life by his sterile aristocratic milieu had taught him something essential about himself. At the time Blok was working on his autobiographical poem *Retribution*, in which he wanted to reflect his complex relationship with his father against the background of the tragic 1905 revolution. Poland—the eternal rebel—is one important setting in the work. In March he wrote the prologue, which comments on the Russian opposition between "fathers" and "sons" and in the "grandsons" glimpses the embryo of a "new human species," "coal" being transformed into "diamond." In Strindberg's work, Blok was already beginning to search for a counterweight to the features of Flaubert's hero that he perceived in his own Russian generation of sons, namely an austerity and tempering that had proved capable of withstanding the test of life. It is from this perspective that his reading of Strindberg left its mark on *Retribution*.

Vladimir Pyast a couple of years before his trip to Stockholm.

In the spring of 1911, Blok and Pyast entertained plans of traveling to Stockholm to visit Strindberg in July. In early June Blok read *By the Open Sea*, after which he wrote to Pyast expressing envy of his friend for having been the first to discover Strindberg: "I truly believe that *now* I find in him that which I *once long ago* found in Shakespeare." The trip, however, was postponed for the time being.

In October, Blok began keeping a diary in an effort to bolster his spirits and endure what he regarded to be Russia's fateful

Aleksandr Blok, 1911.

hour. He feared mental collapse, and thoughts of suicide were never far from his mind. His diary entries describe wanderings in Petersburg's fogs and wind that are reminiscent of Strindberg's walks through Stockholm. He often ventured out into the suburbs and the shores of the Gulf of Finland. His personal drama was closely linked to the city.

From his friend Andrey Bely came letters expressing an increasingly strong sense of imminent catastrophe. Bely was now working on *Petersburg*, which has a great deal in common with *Retribution*. Under the impression of Bely's letters, Blok's depression, if anything, worsened. The crowds on Nevsky Prospekt suddenly seemed to greet him with one and the same horridly cynical "snout" that filled him with terror. At that moment the whole of European culture appeared to be lost, infiltrated by an invisible enemy. He noted in his diary that somewhere in Europe there must be a gaze that can calmly and without fear meet the infernal physiognomies around him. Soon he learned through Bely that Sergey Solovyov, who had just entered a mental clinic, was being haunted and tormented by the same kind of face. It confirmed Blok's impression that the Russian people were incapable of resisting the forces of evil and were dominated by *vyalost'*—flabbiness, impotence, inertia—one of Blok's favorite words.

Soon the diary began to contain more or less veiled attacks against his wife Lyubov, the daughter of chemist Dmitry Mendeleev. Once, ten years earlier, she had been the earthly incarnation of Blok's poetic cult of the World Soul. Now she was increasingly living a life of her own in the theater. Though they were still intimately tied to each other she and Blok had not had sexual relations for several years already.

Blok and Strindberg's Face

In January 1912, Blok jotted down a downright Strindbergian intrigue in his diary that seems to indicate that among other works he had read *A Madman's Manifesto*, in which he was especially likely to have recognized himself, since he too was married to an actress who was trying to emancipate herself. The plot of the novel Blok outlined was modeled on the Mendeleev family's situation. The head of the fictional family is a brilliant scientist who had once fallen in love with "an attractive, feminine, and shallow Swedish woman" (Blok's mother-in-law was half Swedish). In love with his temperament but never seriously loving him, she eventually bears him four children, among them a daughter named Lyubov. After that he abandons her physically, as must "every man" who is interested in advancing socially and becomes absorbed in problems that are inaccessible to women. She begins to mix in society. He dies a few years later. His character and morals have broken down over the years. She—who during their honeymoon was infatuated with him but in the course of their marriage increasingly came to hate him—proclaims his memory to be "sacred," which has to do with the fact that she becomes embroiled in family quarrels over the large estate he left. What, in fact, is to become of her children? There is only one mitigating circumstance—after all, she has no calling, but, as Blok aggressively puts it, is "just a vacuous female."

During one sleepless night and the following morning in late January, Blok read *Inferno*. He had become more or less apathetic, and a physician had diagnosed him as suffering from a "nervous disorder." He refused to see people and even avoided Pyast. That same morning he received a letter asking support from a young woman with whom he had been corresponding. He answered: "To get an idea of the mood I'm in now (and often), you must read Strindberg's trilogy (*A Madman's Manifesto*, *The Son of a Servant*, and *Inferno*)." Significantly, he groups these three "autobiographical" works into a trilogy. He draws no distinction between Strindberg's different roles or stages in life. Strindberg the anti-feminist, the proletarian, the rebellious son, and the occultist are all equally important to him. Yet it is clear that he finds *Inferno* especially relevant, for he sees himself surrounded by mystical signs, murky persecutors, demonic intrigues.

At about this time Bely arrived in Petersburg. Blok lacked the strength to meet him. He said he was utterly "alone": more and more, he stressed, he was living "under the sign of Strindberg." It was not difficult for Bely to understand the meaning of these signals. He replied: "You are of course thinking about *Inferno*. When I read *Inferno* I was deeply shaken when I encountered *my own, innermost* suffering. And I was delighted to learn that I was no longer alone... Strindberg had gone through *the very same experience*." Shortly after this exchange, Blok wrote "How hard it is to wander among men," a poem that became the germ of an entire suite with the Strindbergian title *Dances of Death*, whose all-pervading theme is death in life, a feeling of dissimulation, apathy, emptiness.

In the end Blok felt that he was able to meet Bely after all, and they had an intense six-hour-long conversation. Blok noted later in his diary that he thought what Bely said was "very important." He told Bely about his nervous disorder, the prostitutes, his drinking, and about periodically finding himself defenseless in the power of "the elements." This confession clearly left a mark on Bely's portrayal of the evil shadow worlds that had infiltrated the Russian capital in *Petersburg*. In response to Blok's account of his journey through the inferno and the *"devils"* pursuing him, Bely evoked his growing interest in Theosophy. Given Blok's affinity for Strindberg's occult quest, he hoped for a sympathetic reaction, but Blok was hesitant. His mystical vision was bound up with so much anguish and torment.

Blok was soon planning an article to be entitled "From Ibsen to Strindberg," in which he would describe Ibsen's dramas as a stage in the evolution of Russian Symbolism. With his poetic abstraction, Ibsen was a significant spiritual guide who now had to yield to the concrete Strindberg. In one draft of the article he stated that "We gaze upon Ibsen as an artist from below," whereas "we always look Strindberg straight in the face, as an equal, as one human being looks at another." Ibsen's head is "the head of an enormous bird above the fjords," but Strindberg's is "a human head, a *man's* head; he has a stiff mustache, and his face is lined with deep manly furrows." Ibsen's handshake is "probably the light press of a lion's paw, a white, bloodless hand that forever grasps only the pen," whereas Strindberg's "obviously belongs to a laborer or an athlete." In his hand there is hardly anything loose or soft; it is accustomed to hold both the pen and the crucible, and is marked by sores and boils from his alchemical experiments to produce gold. The occult sciences, theosophy, alchemy, mysticism, all that is hidden, are feared only by minds that are by nature weary, degenerated, one-sided or coarse. Strindberg exemplifies a strong intellect that is not afraid of contradictions. Tolstoy's legacy, for example, is ambiguous—some of his legacy is boring. Strindberg's, in contrast, is joyful rather than depressing.

In April 1912, Blok wrote his article. In it he portrays Ibsen as an eagle that "beckons us to follow, from cliff to cliff" above the Norwegian fjords. Suddenly there is the rumble of an avalanche, the eagle disappears out over the sea, and we find ourselves abandoned in the dark night among the fjords. After undergoing many hardships, however, land is sighted:

> Toward us out of a ravine comes a man with a bitter crease of suffering beneath his stiff mustache and a courageous look in his gray eyes. At last, after the countenance of the eagle, a human face!
> August Strindberg.

Blok uses the adjective *muzhvestvenny* here in its dual meaning of "manly, virile" and "valiant, courageous." Through his manly courage Strindberg has overcome *vyalost'*—flabbiness, feebleness. He is the coal that is being transformed into a diamond.

About then, Blok and Pyast learned that Strindberg had cancer and did not have long to live. They again began planning a trip to Stockholm. Blok, however, was not in any condition to travel, so Pyast set off alone as a correspondent for the daily *Russkoe slovo* (*The Russian Word*). It was urgent for him to try to bid farewell on behalf of them both to "the man who at this time has for me become the most important person and writer on earth."

On April 27, Pyast took the train to Helsingfors and Turku, and he seems to have arrived in Sweden two days later. He booked a room in the Hotel Continental in central Stockholm. He soon learned that Strindberg's daughter Karin and her Russian husband Wladimir Smirnoff were staying at another hotel just a few buildings down. Only an hour and half after his arrival he met with them, reckoning that it was through them that he could best get in touch with the sick man. They told him that Strindberg refused to have visitors. Looking back upon his trip in his memoirs, Pyast recalls that Blok, on his deathbed nine years later, behaved in exactly the same way. Smirnoff told him about the touching solicitude Strindberg showed his relatives from his sickbed, urging them to go to the theater despite his unfortunate situation and even suggesting plays they should see. Smirnoff made it clear to Pyast that there was little hope that Strindberg would recover. A Norwegian Theosophist had recently come to Stockholm and, from an adjoining room if not at Strindberg's bedside, had wanted to "concentrate" on "magnetic" healing, but he was categorically rebuffed. His efforts, however, did not seem as odd to Pyast as they did to a Bolshevik like Smirnoff.

Pyast immediately gave Smirnoff his autobiographical *A Poem in Ninths*, which had appeared in book form the previous year, to take to Strindberg. He notes that in his dedication he tried to put "all the power of our love of someone so dear to us." It is probably this volume that has been preserved in Strindberg's library, with the following German (and parallel Russian) text on the title page: "Nur an August Strindberg, Dem Einzige aber nicht dem Einsame. 29 april 1912. Wl. Pjast" ("Only to August Strindberg, unique but not alone"). His allusion to *Alone* was meant to emphasize that at that moment the Russian Symbolists were with Strindberg, for it was through his confessions in *Alone* that they had found community with him.

Pyast strolled over to Strindberg's "Blue Tower," took a long look at the magical house, and then wandered around the neighborhood. He sat for a while in Tegnérlunden Park and pondered his predicament: "So my whole trip was to come to nothing... I was never to see the man who stands out from all other beings in my view of the world... not look into his eyes, not hear his voice ... no, this was more than I could bear." After long hesitation, he climbed the empty front steps. Mina, the housekeeper, opened the door. Before him he saw the spacious hallway and a half-open door that must have been to Strindberg's sickroom. The apartment was

> Till August Strindberg,
> den Ende, men ny
> redan icke den en-
> same — af unga ryska
> diktare.
>
> Wladimir Pjast,
> skriftställare fr. Ryssland.

Vladimir Pyast's message to Strindberg in a signed envelope.

drab and unpretentious. "So this is how martyrs of science live," he thought, "writers who have themselves chosen isolation." Nothing prevented him from crossing the threshold and looking the dying man in the face. But no—he had already made up his mind not to defy Strindberg's wishes. He left behind yet another copy of *A Poem in Ninths* and a little card in halting Swedish that he evidently attached to it that has been preserved in the Strindberg Museum: "To August Strindberg, unique but now already not alone—from young Russian poets." The card is in an envelope on which he introduced himself as "Wladimir Pjast, writer fr. Russia."

Pyast stayed considerably longer than planned in Stockholm. The article he had sent to Petersburg was eventually published in a different form in the newspaper *Novaya zhizn* (*New Life*). He waited as long as he could for his fee. He stayed in touch the whole time with the Smirnoffs and also met Strindberg's other daughter Greta. Finally, on 10 May, he left for home.

It is interesting to consider Wladimir and Karin Smirnoff's reminiscences of their Russian guest. In his article "August Strindberg's Final Days" (published in the evening daily *Aftontidningen* in 1942) Wladimir (here Vladimir) Smirnoff mentions various eccentrics, among them the Theosophist mentioned above, who had turned up and offered to "heal" the patient with their miracle cures, and it is in that context that he touches on Pyast's visit:

> More remarkable was the fact that a young Russian poet and critic from among the contemporary modernists came all the way from Petersburg hoping to catch a glimpse of the dying writer. He stayed in Stockholm right up to the funeral [here Smirnoff's memory is wrong; M.L.], and since he no more than the others was allowed to come in, he strolled around faithfully outside the Blue Tower, happy to have at least had a chance to see the window and door to the great man's residence. He subsequently published some enthusiastic and sad articles about Strindberg's final days and death in a couple of Petersburg periodicals.

Karin Smirnoff notes in her memoirs:

> First about yet another unusual personality with whom W. and I came into contact in Stockholm at this time. It was a charismatic Russian from Petersburg who came to Stockholm solely out of love and admiration of Strindberg (without ever having met him personally). W. mentions him in his memoirs. He was a young man, a little like Gogol, dark-haired with blue eyes, like the Little Russians. His name was Pestovsky, I have no idea what his first name and patronymic were. He signed himself Pyast, and he seemed to be fairly well-known by that name in poetry and literature circles. . . . I remember P. as a typical "dreamer," as they used to be called, oval face but delicate pale complexion, a high, extremely noble forehead reminiscent of ivory, dark hair—eyes absently "dreamy" and "clairvoyant"—limp handshake, almost reluctant. He spoke softly and in a way that was difficult to understand in sentences that were incomplete or faded off and he neither responded nor listened to what others were saying. I was air to him. At most he would mechanically tilt his head as he looked past me and went on with his own vague chain of thought. We met him several times in Stockholm, sometimes outside as he patrolled Drottninggatan—once in the hotel, when he sought out W. to "ask a few questions" to which he did not seem to expect any answers. . . . P. belonged to the "decadents" headed by the poet Blok, and it was S-g's "mystical works" that appealed to them. They didn't see anything else back then.

Writing here several decades later, Karin Smirnoff is clearly under the influence of her husband, who in another 1942 article on Strindberg ("Reminiscences of a Magnificent Rebel" in the magazine *Vi*) especially emphasized the Russian "decadents'" one-sided attraction to Strindberg's "mystical dramas" and completely overlooked Blok's and Pyast's interest in his political radicalism.

On May 14, Pyast arrived in Petersburg. That evening he visited Blok at home and gave a detailed account of his trip. Blok noted in his diary the following day: "Sad thoughts, everyone close to me is on the brink of insanity; they are sick and unstrung, there has never been a worse time." He added that there was still ice on the Neva, and a cold and damp, thick fog hung over the city. This was the day Strindberg died, but of course Blok knew nothing yet.

On May 16, he was informed that "August Strindberg died the day before yesterday at 16:30." Pyast had visited him that morning and read aloud his unpublished article on Strindberg and Stockholm. Blok noted in his diary that there had been large worker demonstrations in Petersburg the day Strindberg died and that he himself that evening had attended a wrestling match at the circus. Both of these pieces of information have some significance in the context, for he watched wrestling regularly in order to study the athletic bodies that he associated with his dreams of "the new human being."

Over the following six days, Blok wrote a memorial article on Strindberg. On May 23 it was ready, and he submitted it to the journal *Sovremennik* (*The Contemporary*), which featured it in its May issue. "To the Memory of August Strindberg" summarizes what Blok was thinking during the winter and spring, when he was entirely focused on Strindberg. Significantly enough, he takes as his starting point one of the photographs—Herman Hamnqvist's from 1901—that "my friend" brought back from Stockholm. He sits and looks at this portrait as if it were an icon. He contemplates "old August's" proletarian shoulders, his unruly head, his face of a martyr. He pauses to dwell on "the persistent gaze in his stern eyes, before which, it seems, all that is petty, all that is dishonest, that cannot give anything a clear 'yes' or 'no' must fall silent." All in this face "is so dear and so endlessly close to us." Perhaps no one at this moment needs it as much as "we Russians"—Russia's writers in particular. This face is in itself a work of art, a beautiful sculpture that fuses together the utmost simplicity and the utmost complexity, coarse material and gentle spirituality.

Strindberg is just the kind of person that is needed now, Blok goes on: at once artist and human being, creative personality and artisan, a great model that humanity must sooner or later strive to emulate. There is already a certain Goethean quality in Russia, and "we Russians" must similarly look forward with confidence to the day when the soul of the nation will assume "something of the unbending, stern, and festive Strindbergian soul." It is obvious that that in this new century humankind is embarking on new paths. The old soul is breaking, and much old rubbish is being cleared away. During this transitional period, culture has dispatched from its laboratory an "experimental" type of human being. It is obvious from the new literature, with its pathology and pornography and vacillations that engender gloom instead of the will to struggle, that the new human being has yet to be born, that thus far everything is just an untested experiment. Strindberg was one of the first to find himself in the crucible in which culture is shaping a new human species. Fate dogged him with unusual tenacity and subjected him to trials "that a normal person would have found unbearable." He was chosen to be polished so as to approach the future ideal as closely as possible. The material—Strindberg's spirit—has shown itself to be of a rare quality, a harmonious combination of male and female properties, of the principles that thus far have been in imbalance and have hindered humanity's emancipation. When manliness is transformed into masculinity anger becomes spite, when womanliness is transformed into femininity goodness is replaced by sentimentality. Culture wants to recreate manliness and womanliness and bring them closer to each other. For the most part all that have come from such attempts at combination are "neurasthenics," but out of them has also arisen a Strindberg, a "Man" equipped for the new life, which will include a hardening struggle not only between nations but also between the individual and the state. Strindberg was born a democrat. He was obliged to move in plutocratic or aristocratic environments in which he was viewed as a coarse proletarian, a difficult person and a misogynist. However, he was no ordinary male despot. "We," moreover, recognize many of his tendencies "among ourselves." He was harshest toward himself, for he lacked the least trace of sentimentality. His so-called misogyny became his Golgotha. At one time he regarded everything womanly as womanish. That was because he was so courageous, preferring to remain alone with his cruel fate until he could meet a real woman whom his honest and strict spirit could accept.

Strindberg was an artist in this life, Blok summarizes, but in the next he will be just a human being. It is easy to simply call him August, for he seems to invite such a personal form of address. He is a brother and a teacher—a teacher with a special love of science. Most of all, perhaps, he is a *comrade*: with his open and candid gaze and rough and firm handshake, he is so intimately connected with "our" dreams of democracy. The legacy he has bequeathed to coming generations is accessible to everyone; it is a legacy to all *humanity*.

Blok's article was closely related to the "ballet" (or "opera") he had begun working on at the same time, which, when eventually finished in January 1913, became a play entitled *The Rose and the Cross*. On May 27 he sketched it out. The hero of the "ballet" is the knight Bertrand, who loves Chatelaine (later renamed Izora) with an eternal, lofty passion. He is from a simple background, democratically-minded, devoted to his chivalrous ideals. His heart has suffered through many trials and is hardened and honest, but others find him difficult. Chatelaine's "womanish egotism" is flattered by his infatuation, but she is incapable of requiting his love. She flirts and teases and knows how to lead him on. The "ballet" has obvious autobiographical roots, for Bertrand has traits of both Blok and Pyast. At the same time, he is consistent in all essentials with Blok's portrait of Strindberg.

On his wife's initiative, Blok soon invested his own and her inherited money in a theater workshop in Terijoki that summer, which was to culminate in a Strindberg production as a posthumous tribute to him. It gave Lyubov Blok a chance to make a comeback after several years' absence. The project was also planned to be a democratic demonstration. Staging plays in the Grand Duchy of Finland made it possible to bypass the Russian censorship, which was important not least as a matter of principle. The project was to be carried out "in the spirit of Finnish independence," as Pyast describes it in his memoirs, and at the same time was meant to link Petersburg Symbolism closer to Sweden and thus to Strindberg. It marked the beginning of what Pyast calls his and Blok's "Strindberg summer." "That Finland was a 'filial of Sweden' was something we soon saw for ourselves," he adds. Many Petersburg intellectuals had summer homes in the seaside resorts on the Gulf of Finland, and besides the local Finnish population there were also many Swedes.

Lyubov Blok recruited her actor friends Aleksandr Mgebrov (who would eventually become a prominent name on the Russian stage) and Valentina Verigina for the project. Vsevolod Meyerhold was contracted as director and Nikolay Kulbin as chief stage designer, assisted by Nikolay Sapunov, a friend of Blok's who had previously closely collaborated with Meyerhold. Boris Pronin was appointed the overall administrator of the undertaking. Kulbin and Pronin, as well as the other actors in the troupe, were recruited from the circles around the Brodyachaya Sobaka cabaret, which since it opened in January 1912 had quickly become a center of cultural life in the capital. Pronin was the founder of the cabaret and Kulbin more or less the driving force behind it. That spring the pair had organized a number of cabarets and improvised poetry readings in its basement premises. Blok rented a small theater in the Casino Hotel in Terijoki from Viktor Junker, a young Finland Swede, and a roomy house on the shore for the actors. Proudly named "The Terijoki Theater of the Association of Actors, Artists, Writers, and Musicians," the troupe gathered there in early June and began preparations. Blok, however, remained in Petersburg. They agreed to stage *There are Crimes and Crimes* (its Russian title was *Guilty or Innocent*) in late July.

Blok commissioned Kulbin to do a large portrait of Strindberg for the premiere, for "old August's" face naturally had to be present at this memorial production. Kulbin was given all of the Strindberg postcards Pyast had brought back from Stockholm. He intended to create a "synthetic" portrait from the personality traits Blok had pointed out in his article. Synthesis was a central notion for Kulbin. He was an almost unlikely representative of the Russian avant-garde during this transitional period between Symbolism and Futurism, when the two movements were still able to get along. Known as "the crazy doctor," the extremism he exemplified was a cheerful, explosive Cubo-Futurist position distinct from that of Blok and his Symbolist friends. On the one hand he was a physician attached to the General Staff and a Privatdozent (Associate Professor) at the Academy of Military Medicine, while on the other he was an indefatigable propagandist for everything novel and experimental in art, literature, and music, and was an arranger of exhibitions, publisher, and theorist as well. Over the course of the next few years he would do a series of charcoal and lithograph portraits that are perhaps the most important part of his legacy.

Nikolay Kulbin's portrait of Strindberg, 1912.

There is a remarkable psychological dynamic in Kulbin's picture in which distinct features are rendered with minimal means. Strindberg's face may in fact mark the beginning of his entire suite of portraits. He did not have a living model, so his Strindberg hardly compares with the others, but he definitely succeeded in conveying something of what Blok wanted to bring out: maturity, a union of intimacy and coarseness, complexity and simplicity. Working in a modified Cubist idiom, he based himself primarily on Richard Bergh's painting. Unfortunately, Kulbin's original has not been preserved, but it was published before the opening night of the play in Terijoki in the June issue of the journal *Novaya studiya* (*The New Studio*).

Blok went on living amid his visions. When he learned that Greta Strindberg was killed in a serious railroad accident, he interpreted it mystically: "The old man called her home," Pyast remembers him saying. In his diary entry of June 24, he notes that "the horrors of life have been following me for five days now." Two days later he sent two portraits of Strindberg to the eccentric prosaist Aleksey Remizov, a friend who was also in poor psychic condition, as though in an effort to cure him. The next evening, Sapunov, with whom Blok had become especially close, drowned at Terijoki. It almost seemed to be a kind of suicide. Blok complained that his own nerves were overwrought. His marital problems had become even worse when he found out that his wife had begun an affair with a young actor in Meyerhold's company.

On July 27 the memorial performance was held in the Terijoki theater. The audience consisted of many Finns and Swedes and Petersburg intellectuals. Wladimir and Karin Smirnoff arrived from Helsingfors on special invitation. In front of a stage bestrewn with ferns, Pyast opened the evening with a talk on Strindberg. Kulbin's portrait stood on the proscenium, and the entire stage was bordered in black. In retrospect, the production stands out as one of Meyerhold's most exciting Symbolist experiments. Utilizing musical and rhythmic techniques, the staging featured crisp, cold dialogue, prolonged pauses, stiff movement patterns, and red, yellow, and black color stylizations in the scenery and costumes. Meyerhold had expressly forbidden elasticity and modulation. Kulbin's young assistant Yury Bondi was responsible for the scenery, and the lead roles of Maurice, Henriette, and Jeanne were played by Mgebrov, Verigina, and Lyubov Blok, respectively. The actors, who mostly kept to the rear half of the stage, occasionally appeared against the bluish-black transparent background to be almost immobile silhouettes.

Perhaps the most powerful scene was Maurice and Henriette's meeting in the Luxembourg Gardens. The place itself was merely suggested as shadowed branches in a golden dusk light. Maurice wore a dark suit, his mistress Henriette a red coat. They sat in stiff poses on a bench and exchanged their lines as though they were rapier thrusts. Blok found parts of the production brilliant, among them this scene. He thought that the yellow twilight and bright red coat effectively underscored the veiled threat in the play. Another scene that made a deep impression on him was the first meeting between Maurice and Henriette in the restaurant.

Henriette's silent entry gave the audience an early hint of what was to come. Maurice watched her from the bar. She walked around in a figure eight without looking in his direction. "This is how you'll immediately trap him," Meyerhold had instructed Verigina. Henriette carried a bouquet of red flowers, and all her attention seemed to be focused on them. This was one of the long pauses, or "cries of silence," that the director had scattered into the play. On one occasion, Henriette grabbed one of the gloves Maurice's wife Jeanne had given him as a present and shoved it into his champagne glass. Meyerhold incorporated into the play several pregnant gestures such as this, which complemented the hard, metallic verbal exchanges.

Contrasting with the meetings between Maurice and Henriette was Jeanne's quiet grief. Her entire being breathed restrained anxiety and pent-up tenderness as she stooped, almost immobile and lost in pain over her little daughter's grave in the cemetery. One viewer, who was herself a member of the troupe, confessed to Verigina that this scene had moved her so deeply that she could still clearly see it fifty years later.

The performance had a profound effect on Blok, who associated it with his reading of *Inferno*. The guilt and muffled threat that the play conveyed was what he himself felt. It was not difficult for him to identify with the playwright Maurice. He probably also perceived traits of his wife both in Henriette (the "coquette," as he calls her), who as a sculptress had an artistic profession and was emphatically independent in her lifestyle, and in Maurice's abandoned wife Jeanne, grieving over her lost child. Surely contributing to the unusual affinity Lyubov felt for the role was the fact that three years earlier she had herself lost a newborn baby. Although it was not Blok's, he had regarded it as his own and had mourned it in a poem.

Blok had the opportunity to meet the Smirnoffs in connection with the performance. It pained him not to be able to say anything to Karin in either Swedish or German. According to what he reported to his mother in a letter, he found her "a very tall, thin, middle-aged woman in a three-cornered hat with a white feather, simply dressed." She resembled her father "in the very best way." She complimented him on his wife's acting, which she said surpassed that of a Helsinki actress she had seen. Pyast noted that the Smirnoffs praised the entire production, claiming that they had never seen a better version: "Just like that, with that kind of scenery, is how Strindberg should be performed." Pyast was especially interested in their opinion of Kulbin's "masterpiece," and was delighted to hear that they considered the portrait a very faithful resemblance, perhaps even the best of its kind. Verigina remembers them spontaneously asking: "Is it really possible that such a remarkable performance cannot be staged in Petersburg?"

Wladimir Smirnoff briefly comments on the memorial evening in Terijoki in his article "Reminiscences of a Magnificent Rebel":

> I myself had an opportunity to attend a unique tribute to Strindberg's memory the summer after his death at which the famous Russian poet Alexander Block [sic; M.L.] was also present. It was in a garden suburb near Petersburg, where a Russian theater company in which Mrs. Block was an actress, performed *There are Crimes and Crimes*. The performance was preceded by a commemorative speech delivered in a subdued tone at a table covered in a black velvet cloth and two lighted wax candles.

In her memoir notes written some 50 years later, Karin Smirnoff summarizes her impressions as follows:

> After Papa's death—before we traveled to Loviisa, Pestovski invited Wladimir and me to Terijoki, where a group of theater artists (some of them amateurs) and writers had settled down for the summer in a very large but half-dilapidated "dacha" with almost no furniture, no curtains, meagerly equipped with washstands, dirty wallpaper, poor iron bedsteads, and mismatched chairs. They were supposed to hold a memorial evening in S-g's honor.

Blok and Strindberg's Face

We arrived on a morning train toward evening and were immediately surrounded by polite but very quiet and reverent "artists" who didn't exactly know whether or not they should express condolences and mumbled and shook hands with us. Alexander Blok stayed the longest with us, while the others disappeared into the interior of the house, after enthusiastically pointing out that Blok was the poet Blok, whom they deeply admired. He wrote "symbolically," as it was called at the time.

After a while they took us to a hall with an improvised stage. They were to perform an act from *There are Crimes and Crimes*, the scene on the bench in the park, if I remember correctly. It turned out to be very Russian. (Note: Mrs. Blok was an actress and played the lead role.) But before the curtain was opened Pyast stood behind a table covered in a velvet cloth all the way to the floor and talked about S-g. Then a poem by Blok about S-g was read, and then came the play. After the performance we were led up to a half-length portrait of S-g (based on Richard Bergh's painting, it seemed) in black and white with a triangular nose, square cheeks, etc. I wanted to laugh and said nothing, but Wladimir was polite and mumbled again and again "Ochen interesno, ochen interesno...." (Very interesting, very interesting) without finding anything else to say, which made me want to laugh even harder, all the more so since we were once again surrounded by the silent artists, who stared at us expectantly. Blok (note: at the time admired by the "decadents," after the first revolution even more deified by the revolutionaries, died 1920 or '21), who noticed that we were not very sympathetic, explained that "it wasn't a question of a portrait in the strict sense, but....," etc., but Papa's large, round, coal-black eyes looking out from all the triangles and squares kept me from following the symbolic explanation.

Two cultures are colliding here. Karin Smirnoff has attended one of the most original productions of Russian Symbolism, a memorial performance dedicated to her father that to the circle of Petersburg artists suggested a sacred ritual, with Strindberg mystically present in the room. She describes the event from a coolly ironic distance as an "act" (it is of course significant that what she remembers is the scene in the Luxembourg Gardens) performed more or less by amateurs running a cult of the "decadent" Blok. Keeping this in mind, there is reason to question the degree to which the Smirnoffs' attitude toward the performance, as unanimously remembered by Blok, Pyast, and Verigina at various points in time, might be just their misinterpretation of their guests' polite niceties.

The next day, June 28, which was hot and muggy with the threat of a thunderstorm, Blok set himself to summarize his overwhelming impressions of Terijoki in a letter to his mother. He notes that he was for the first time impressed with Lyubov as an actress. She stood in the church in the first scene with the baby in her arms and uttered words "full of dreadful premonitions," and she finally did so "in her own very powerful and expressive voice, which is especially well suited to Strindberg's language." Blok was quite struck by this language: "It is simplicity taken to frightening dimensions: the life of the soul translated into the language of mathematical formulae, and these formulae are in turn rendered through conditional signs reminiscent of streaks of lightning zigzagging over a very black cloud; during those years Strindberg spoke exclusively the language of lightning; the world surrounding him then was like a thundercloud in July, a tabula rasa on which the lightning of his will could draw any zigzag patterns whatever." He adds that suddenly, "into the café scene," which had an almost absurd feeling to it, had crept features of the Sophocles drama, with the police superintendent in the role of the messenger of the antique tragedy: "Nothing except bluish-black and red. Such are Sophocles and Strindberg."

In August, Blok stressed in a letter to Emilii Medtner that Strindberg was so close to "us" because he was prepared to measure everything with the "ultimate" standards without ever fearing to be ridiculous. "Not an inch" had he yielded to aestheticism when it really mattered.

In October, Blok attended the opening of Kulbin's major exhibition of his works in downtown Petersburg. It featured Strindberg's portrait for the first—and as far as we know only— time. Toward the end of the month Blok wrote "Night. Street. Lamp. Pharmacy," a poem lamenting the meaningless repetitiveness of life, which he incorporated into the cycle of poems "The Dances of

Death." It seems to echo the notion of existence as eternal martyrdom in *The Dance of Death*.

Blok's passion for Strindberg had climaxed that summer, as had his friendship with Pyast. "Old August" continued to be present in his consciousness, albeit not as intensely. In 1913 he jotted down "There is a Game," a poem that arouses associations with Strindberg's theme of persecution. In 1914 he dedicated another poem, "A Woman," to the memory of Strindberg. In his article "The Decline of Humanism" written five years later, after viewing the Bolshevik revolution as a mystical act of purification, he described the life of the nineteenth-century artist as "unbearable." As was especially clear from Strindberg's portrayal of how he had been "tortured" with the most refined, occult methods, the artist had allowed himself to be hounded and tormented.

Still, Strindberg helped Blok survive 1911 and 1912. It was only with the "Strindberg icon" before him that he managed to make his way through the darkness that in those years seemed to be descending over Russia.

THE EARLY BREAKTHROUGH OF PSYCHOANALYSIS IN RUSSIA

Nowhere outside the centers of German-speaking Europe in Vienna and Zurich did psychoanalysis achieve such an early and broad breakthrough as in Russia. Over the course of a few years around 1910, deep psychology and Russian culture seem to have had an intense need for each other. Russia was working through its disappointment over the Revolution of 1905, and the new psychodynamic theory was evolving into its different variants. Under these conditions a remarkable cross-fertilization took place. By 1914, in fact, everything Sigmund Freud had written thus far had already been translated into Russian.

The first breakthrough year was 1909, when Freudian theory was described in detail in the two leading Russian psychiatric publications *Zhurnal nevropatologii i psikhiatrii* (*Journal of Neuropathology and Psychiatry*) and *Sovremennaya psikhiatriya* (*Modern Psychiatry*). The former featured an article by Dr. Nikolay Vyrubov entitled "Freud's Psychoanalytical Method and its Therapeutic Significance," in which he reported on his own experiences with the new therapy at the Kryukovo Sanatorium that he headed, while the latter carried a contribution in two sections by Dr. Osip Feltsman entitled "On Psychoanalysis and Psychotherapy" describing his own application of Freud's method. A report from Zurich in *Sovremennaya psikhiatriya* detailed a fascinating case of a female Russian-Jewish patient successfully treated by Carl Gustav Jung at Burghölzli. She was Sabina Spielrein, Jung's Freudian "experimental case," who at this time was herself studying to become an analyst and was involved in a complex romantic relationship with her former therapist.

The Early Breakthrough of Psychoanalysis in Russia

Pioneers of Psychoanalysis:
Osip Feltsman, 1912, Nikolay Vyrubov, 1912, and Nikolay Osipov, 1914.

Also in 1909, together with his colleagues Nikolay Osipov, Aleksandr Bernstein, and Yury Kannabikh, Dr. Vyrubov was planning to publish a bi-monthly journal, to be called *Psikhoterapiya*, which would be devoted exclusively to the new therapeutic ideas, especially psychoanalysis and the likewise much discussed "persuasive" method of Dr. Paul Dubois. Osipov, who was the driving force behind the project, had received his medical degree in Switzerland; almost all the leading Russian psychiatrists, in fact, had studied or practiced in German-speaking countries. In 1907 he had visited Jung at Burghölzli, and shortly thereafter he had worked with Jungian association tests as an assistant at the Moscow University Psychiatric Clinic. He also contributed many articles on psychoanalysis to the journals, particularly reviews and summaries of Freud's works, some of the originals of which he and Dr. Feltsman planned to publish in Russian in a special series.

Osipov was also the spirit behind the "little Fridays" at the University Clinic devoted to discussion of the new psychodynamic ideas, so named in contrast to the "big" Friday gatherings organized by the official Neuropathology and Psychiatry Society. At about this time the Society announced a contest for the best essay on the theme "The Psychoanalysis of Freud and Others in the Treatment of Functional Nervous Disorders." In December 1909, Osipov wrote to Freud personally to schedule a visit, which took place in

June 1910. He made a very good impression on Freud, who sent an enthusiastic report on their meeting to his colleague Sándor Ferenczi in Budapest.

The first issue of *Psikhoterapiya* appeared in February 1910, six months before Freud's own journal *Zentralblatt für Psychoanalyse*, which was under the editorship of Alfred Adler and Wilhelm Stekel. Osipov was also on the editorial board of *Zentralblatt*, which guaranteed collaboration between the two publications. Another member of the board was Dr. Moisey Vulf (Moshe Woolf) from Odessa, who had introduced psychotherapy there in the local journal *Terapevticheskoe obozrenie* (*Therapeutic Review*) and had corresponded with Freud at about the same time as Osipov. It was not least through his efforts that Odessa soon followed Moscow to become the second center of deep psychology in Russia.

Psikhoterapiya now began publishing original articles, reviews and summaries, and before long it had developed a thoroughly psychoanalytical profile. Beginning in 1911, it also started to feature translations. Editor-in-chief Vyrubov and his wife translated many of Freud's shorter works. 1911-1912 also saw the translation into Russian of many of Freud's other writings. Vyrubov started his own series based on the journal translations, as did Vulf in Odessa. At about this time in Vienna both Vulf, who was visiting, and Sabina Spielrein, who arrived from Zurich, joined the Psychoanalytical Society. In November 1911, Spielrein presented there an excerpt from her article "Destruction as the Cause of Coming into Being," which inspired Freud's later theory of the death drive.

One could call 1912 the second and more definitive breakthrough year of psychoanalysis in Russia. In February 1911, after Osipov and some 130 professors and lecturers left the University to protest the government's repressive cultural policies, the "little Fridays" at the Moscow University Clinic were established as an independent forum. Attended by psychiatrists, pedagogues, and criminologists for discussions of the new psychotherapy, as early as March 1912 these open gatherings regularly attracted some 60 visitors. Aesthetic issues came up as well, for Kannabikh, Vyrubov, and Osipov, who organized the meetings, also had literary interests in common. Kannabikh wrote and even published

The Early Breakthrough of Psychoanalysis in Russia

Sigmund Freud among Russians.
On his left, Max Eitingon, on the right, Moisey Vulf.

prose, while Osipov was working on a major Freudian study of Tolstoy, fragments of which appeared in *Psikhoterapiya*. In Osipov's interpretation, his works of fiction were primarily a stage in the writer's mental self-healing process.

The rapid spread of psychoanalysis in Russia is best understood in the light of the abortive Revolution of 1905 and the intelligentsia's psychic and moral crises in the wake of the increasingly repressive policies of the state. Freud's theory of neurosis proved valuable in coping with this situation. Many of the Russian doctors had a revolutionary past themselves, and, notably, many of them were Jews. Especially the cathartic and dynamic elements in Freud's method and personality theory seemed to speak directly to them. Yet at the same time they found it difficult to accept Freud's limitations and considered that his theories needed to be complemented in essential respects by the work of Alfred Adler, who attributed less significance to the instincts and took greater account of the role of social factors. Various objections to Freud's sexual dogma had been raised as early as 1909, for example, in Feltsman's introductory article in *Sovremennaya psikhiatriya*. Adler was himself a Social Democrat who had been deeply influenced by socially conscious Russian literature and the Russian intellectuals who went "to the people" in the 1870s. He had visited Russia together with his radical Russian Jewish wife, and through her had early on established contact with Mensheviks in Vienna, including Lev Trotsky.

Sergey Pankeev, the Wolfman, circa 1910.

As Freudianism entered its second breakthrough phase in Russia, *Psikhoterapiya* began opening its pages to presentations of work Adler was doing on inferiority complexes and the aggressive will to power as the basis of neurosis. Vyrubov even joined Adler's newly founded society for "free psychoanalytical research," which was eventually renamed as the Society for Individual Psychology. When Freud broke with *Zentralblatt* in late 1912, the single remaining editor, Wilhelm Stekel, was actively supported by Adler in his effort to bind the journal even closer to *Psikhoterapiya* in Moscow through agreements providing for more extensive collaboration and exchanges of articles between the two publications. Adler and Stekel and a number of Adler's Russian and non-Russian followers from Odessa, Vienna, Budapest, Zurich, Basel, and Geneva soon joined the permanent staff of *Psikhoterapiya*. At the same time, the journal declared that it would continue to write "accurately" about Freud and would translate his works alongside those of Adler. The ideas of the two men were quite simply never considered to be as antagonistic in Russia as was the case in Vienna.

Adler's fascination with Russian literature inspired his twenty-one year-old colleague Otto Kaus, who was also deeply interested in Russia, to publish in 1912 an Adlerian study of Gogol—*The Gogol Case*—in a newly founded series. Otherwise, Adler's favorite author was Dostoevsky, and one wonders to what extent the Russian writer's criminal psychology may have influenced his own theory. In 1913 he urged Kaus, who by then was also on the staff of *Psikhoterapiya*, to write what he hoped would be a major study of Dostoevsky. The meetings of Adler's Society for Individual Psychology now very frequently addressed literary analyses regularly surveyed in *Psikhoterapiya* by Raisa Adler.

This was the state of affairs when a Russian became Freud's most famous patient. In February 1910, Sergey Pankeev, eventually to be known as the "Wolfman," arrived from Odessa for a consultation. With him was Leonid Droznes, an Odessan psychiatrist who, as early as the summer of 1909, shortly after Dr. Vulf's article in *Terapevticheskoe obozrenie*, had attempted to treat Pankeev with psychoanalysis. As James Rice notes in *Freud's Russia*, he was "made to order" for Freud at this particular moment in 1910. Although he spoke almost fluent German, to Freud he exemplified a Russian national character with strong archaic vestiges that were manifested not least in a profound emotional ambivalence. These features seemed to enable Freud to penetrate deeper than anyone before him into the primitive strata of the personality and early childhood experiences to lay bare what he called the "primal trauma" (Urtrauma) of the afflicted psyche.

Freud had become interested in Russia early on, which perhaps had to do with the fact that he had grown up in a Slavic linguistic milieu in Moravia. He had been close friends with a couple of Russian fellow students when he studied with Jean Martin Charcot in Paris, and had co-authored a study on brain anatomy with one of them. His own mother had spent some important childhood years in Odessa, while one of his uncles had business ties to the city and had occasionally traveled there. The first foreign physician interested in psychoanalysis to come forward in Vienna was the Russian-born Max Eitingon, with whom Freud soon established a life-long friendship.

As Freud's analysis would conclude, Sergey Pankeev's father was the overshadowing Oedipal figure in his son's case history, an object of Sergey's "excessive love" and the source of his intense fear of castration. Freud briefly describes the father's life in his case study as "rich in events and experiences." Konstantin Pankeev was in fact one of the wealthiest men in southern Russia, a landowner, left-liberal politician, and patron of the arts. Freud's description, which was intentionally vague to avoid revealing the subject's identity, says nothing about the significant role he played in Russia early in the century. His social involvement was quite simply of no interest to an investigation of an "infantile neurosis," nor was the politically indifferent Freud capable of evaluating it. Freud mentions the adult Sergey's continued rivalry with his sister—his father's favorite and his "seductress" at an early age—but says not a word about his patient's jealousy of Pankeev Sr.'s political activities, which in fact seem to have had a bearing on the affliction he contracted in adolescence.

As Freud also notes, Konstantin Pankeev had been diagnosed as manic depressive. As in the case of Aleksey Venkstern, his illness seems to have fluctuated in close conformity with shifting political events in Russia. In his youth around 1880, he had gone "to the people" in the spirit of the age, an act that was all the more remarkable in that he was a millionaire. A few years after his son was born in 1886, he sank into depression, at the same time that political stagnation tightened its grip on Russia. In the years immediately preceding the 1905 Revolution he became almost maniacally active. In the summer of 1903 he participated in the historic meeting at Lake Constance (Bodensee), where liberals like himself and ex-Marxist intellectuals founded the so called Union of Liberation. He came incognito to avoid police surveillance, and arranged to issue advice and instructions for continued underground political activity in southern Russia. Beginning in the autumn of that year, he edited the Odessa journal *Yuzhnye zapiski* (*Southern Notes*), which he quickly attempted to make a center of political radicalism. In 1904, he donated a large sum of money (30,000 rubles) to "centralized terrorism," immediately after the reactionary Minister of the Interior Plehve was killed by a bomb in the middle of Petersburg. It was at this time that his son appears to have entered the apathetic state that would eventually bring him to Freud.

In the revolutionary autumn of 1905, the Pankeev home in Odessa seems to have become a debate club under the surveillance of the police, and a stream of brochures, proclamations, posters, and fliers issued from the offices of his periodical. Pankeev also helped found the Constitutional Democrat Party—the so called Kadets. He was elected to the Duma but withdrew to preserve his anonymity. His son reacted to all this by hobnobbing with young monarchists. Pankeev Sr. was dealt a heavy double blow in 1906, when the Revolution was crushed and his beloved daughter committed

The Early Breakthrough of Psychoanalysis in Russia

"Little Friday" meeting at the Moscow University Psychiatric Clinic in April 1911. In the middle row on the far right Nikolay Osipov, Mikhail Asatiani, and Osip Feltsman. Third from the left in the front row, dean of Russian psychiatry Vladimir Serbsky.

suicide. With his wife he began planning to make a large donation in her memory to a clinic in Odessa. He simultaneously initiated his most ambitious political and cultural undertaking, the Petersburg miscellany *Zarnitsy* (*Summer Lightning*), which was intended to illuminate the Russian gloom. His idea was to use his extensive network of contacts to gather the entire leftist intelligentsia (except the Bolsheviks) to embark upon a joint project. Writers, politicians, scholars, and journalists would be given an opportunity to describe and analyze the contemporary situation. Contributors included Ivan Bunin, Aleksandr Kuprin, and a number of prominent liberals. At this same time, Sergey slipped deeper and deeper into depression. By the time the first issue of *Zarnitsy* appeared in the spring of 1908, Konstantin Pankeev had already brought his son for hypnosis therapy to his friend Vladimir Bekhterev, the best known neurologist in Russia and one of the country's most prominent leftist personages. He put even more effort into the next volume, but in July 1908 he died suddenly of aortic stenosis at the age of fifty. The second and last issue of *Zarnitsy*, a volume of over 500 pages, appeared in early 1909. Thus it was only a short while later, when various treatments at German sanatoria had proved ineffective, that Droznes began experimenting with psychoanalysis on the apathetic Sergey.

It is not surprising that Sergey Pankeev should have immediately decided to stay with Freud. A year and a half after his father's death, he found in Freud an ideal paternal surrogate, a revolutionary of the psyche, an "explorer," as he himself called him, out to conquer a new world. And in this historic mission of his, Freud chose not to reject his "son." On the contrary, he took him into his confidence as a colleague and even focused his research on *his own* personality. Sergey, moreover, had grown up in a strongly Judeophile environment, for his father had been deeply involved in the Jewish question. Except for the war years, Sergey remained in Vienna the rest of his life, in contact throughout with psychoanalytic circles.

Thus, Sergey Pankeev had grown up in a genuinely literary environment and had personally met writers and journalists in his own home. It seems natural, therefore, that his memoirs should report that he and Freud often touched upon Russian literature in their conversations. Freud made clear that his fascination with Mikhail Lermontov, who was killed in a duel at an early age, was connected with his unexpressed grief over the death of his sister. They discussed in particular Dostoevsky, whom Freud evidently used extensively as a template in his approach to Pankeev and the Russian psyche. It seems significant that precisely in 1910, the first year of the analysis, Freud purchased not only Dostoevsky's complete works in 22 volumes, but also Dmitry Merezhkovsky's study *Tolstoy and Dostoevsky*. James Rice suggests that Dostoevsky's unique autobiographical story "The Peasant Marey" may have influenced Pankeev's treatment. That work describes Dostoevsky's fear of wolves as a child, and it seems to conform very well to Freud's interpretation of Dostoevsky in his later essay and of Pankeev as a latent homosexual in love with his paternal authorities, who alternately rebelled against and bowed down before the tsar and

God. Freud considered *The Brothers Karamazov* the best novel ever written, and its role in the analysis had to do with the fact that Pankeev recognized Karamazovian features in his own family. Another topic of discussion was Merezhkovsky's novel *Peter and Aleksey*, which describes how Peter the Great had his son killed for opposing his reforms. The work was relevant to Pankeev's identification with the tsarevich, and it was also one of Freud's favorite novels. We can surmise that it was very easy for Pankeev to project his father's features onto the revolutionary Tsar Peter.

It is worth noting that as Freud was conducting his analysis of Pankeev, Bely was digging into the Russian trauma of parricide in *Petersburg*, taking both *The Brothers Karamazov* and *Peter and Aleksey* as equally central points of departure. Bely was not very familiar with Freud's theories, but they were in the air all around him. As we have seen, his friend Sergey Solovyov underwent psychoanalytical therapy with Kannabikh, and another friend, Emilii Medtner, soon consulted Freud directly.

Over the course of 1914, the philosopher Ivan Ilyin and Medtner went through analysis with Freud and Jung, respectively. Their therapies, which resulted directly from the breakthrough of psychoanalysis in Russia, deserve separate treatment.

Anthroposophy's Decade in Russia

In 1912-1913, the Symbolists drew closer to Rudolf Steiner and the emerging Anthroposophy movement. Their own movement had foundered, and it was in that situation that Steiner took on such importance for Russian writers and thinkers.

Steiner's thought had a great deal in common with the philosophy of Vladimir Solovyov. His doctrine, which proclaims that through a series of incarnations we can perfect ourselves as spiritual beings and ultimately attain union with Christ, seemed essentially in harmony with Solovyov's early prophecy that modern humans would be transformed into "God-men." When Steiner broke with Theosophy and its focus on Hinduism and Buddhism and restored a Western foundation to esotericism by positing the mystery of Golgotha as the goal of history, he also became more interested than previously in Russia, which was situated on the boundary between Oriental and Occidental cultures. He was inclined to attribute to Russia a crucial significance for the future of humanity, a notion that was close to the old Slavophile idea, as elaborated particularly by Dostoevsky, of Russia's Christian mission in the world.

In May 1912, Andrey Bely heard Steiner speak in Cologne on "Christ in the Twentieth Century." It was an overwhelming experience that changed his life. He decided to undergo occult training in Munich and sent a number of letters to his friends in which he attempted to convince them that only Steiner could give humanity the answer it needed in the midst of its fateful crisis. Among his Symbolist friends, Ellis had become a Steiner adherent the previous year. What Bely felt he had to do now was to lead his poet colleagues Blok and Vyacheslav Ivanov—as well as philosophers in the Symbolist periphery such as Nikolay Berdyaev and Sergey Bulgakov—"to insight."

Bely was soon sending Blok excited reports in which he laid special emphasis on Steiner's enormous charisma. These accounts undoubtedly had an effect on Blok, although at the time he was looking to August Strindberg for support. When, little by little, Bely attempted in his letters to interpret Blok's poetic evolution in "spiritual scientific" terms, and claimed that he knew a way out of their torment and how to return to their expectations at the turn of the century, Blok was naturally obliged to listen.

Ivanov, who besides his poetry had, like Bely, aspired to lay the foundation of a symbolistic aesthetic-philosophical theory, was also likely to be deeply impressed by Bely's letters. As early as September 1912, he traveled to Basel (where Steiner was scheduled to lecture) to try to join the German division of the Theosophical Society, which at its recently concluded congress in Munich had for the first time declared its independence vis-à-vis the Society's center in India. Remarkably enough, however, Steiner advised him against membership—perhaps because of Ivanov's excessively self-indulgent artistic temperament, perhaps owing to the extremely strong emphasis he placed on the ecstatic Dionysian element in his symbolistic doctrine. Bely was also in Basel, however, and he and Ivanov had some serious discussions of Nietzsche (who had been active and in fact fallen mentally ill there) and the future of Russia and Symbolism.

As for Sergey Bulgakov, the religious philosopher who after the October revolution became an Orthodox priest, Bely had spoken with him about Steiner in Moscow in April 1912, shortly before they met again in Cologne. Bulgakov had reacted very negatively and warned against "German rationalism." Bulgakov's friend Berdyaev, on the other hand, had a different opinion of Steiner, as is evident from two letters he wrote in response to Bely in June and December 1912. There he was basically ambivalent toward spiritual science, which both attracted and repelled him. Actually, this dual attitude toward Steiner seems more or less typical of all the Russian Symbolists (including Bely himself, although he tried to

Rudolf Steiner, 1916.

conceal it behind a veil of overwrought hyperbole and by relieving some of his inner tensions in *Petersburg*).

What did Berdyaev have to say on the subject? His philosophy had points in common with Ivanov's. It was apocalyptic, stressed the revolutionary significance to the personality of creative ecstasy, and prophesied about the emergence of a new cosmic consciousness in the twentieth century. It is thus not difficult to understand the allure that Steiner must have had for Berdyaev. He admits in his first letter to Bely that for several years he had found Steiner's public appearances "troubling." He had read everything he came over of Steiner's writings but found his popular pedagogical style annoying. Deep within, however, he seemed to detect something significant. If he had the possibility, he went on, he would travel to Munich, where Steiner's colony was at the time, and observe the spiritual scientist at close quarters. Like other religious philosophers close to the Symbolists, Berdyaev had distanced himself from the Orthodox Church, but now during the decline of the movement he had returned. Why is Christ not more central to Steiner's doctrine, he asks. Why is it incumbent exclusively on us humans to train our personalities to attain cosmic clairvoyance; why is the miracle of reconciliation absent? Why, to put it succinctly, "does not a single sunbeam ever fall from above onto our path?" Steiner had no basic Christology, in Berdyaev's opinion. The initiation he showed was all too deeply influenced by the materialistic notion of evolution and all too little reminiscent of divine grace and the mystical union through Christ.

Berdyaev's second objection has to do with the Dionysian element of life. Why did Steiner attribute so much power to reason; why did he not recognize the value of instinct and passion, and the entire subconscious sphere of the personality? The third and final question deals with the human creative power, which is the core of Berdyaev's own philosophy. He wonders whether Steiner's prescriptions for initiation might be an appeal for passivity, and whether they might simply mean that the spiritual scientist is initiated into the static wisdom of past millennia. He emphasizes that there is a dynamic in the moment of creation that the ancient sages were never capable of attaining.

Nikolay Berdyaev, 1912.

Berdyaev's December 1912 letter to Bely (whose response, unfortunately, has been lost) is shorter but more emphatically expresses his appreciation of Steiner. He reports that Ivanov, who had returned Russia, even accused him of being too strongly attracted to the Steiner adherents among the Symbolists. He goes on to say that over the summer and fall he has read a lot about Steiner and has understood a great deal and reassessed other things. Although he cannot become a devotee, he realizes Steiner's "colossal" historical significance as a symptom of an approaching universal upheaval that neither the Church nor science is capable of envisaging. He says that he feels the physical dimension of life being rocked to its foundations, and that only a new consciousness can save humanity from the cosmic wind that has begun to blow. Steiner's occult clairvoyance alone, however, cannot liberate us: we must also try to find our bearings in the "whirlwind" through the Cross, by coming to know Christ better.

While some Symbolists around this time followed in Bely's footsteps and committed themselves to Steiner, Blok, Ivanov, and Bulgakov became increasingly critical. Blok was influenced to a certain extent by Emilii Medtner, who attempted to convince him of Steiner's philosophical shallowness and warned that occult meditation could have a deteriorating effect on the artistic imagination.

As Bely successively broke away from the Musagetes publishing house headed by Medtner, the latter was pushed toward a psychic precipice as he watched his entire project capsize. He began working on *Reflections of Goethe*, a polemical pamphlet against Steiner in which he argued that for his own obscure purposes, the "pastor of Anthroposophy" had appropriated the Goethe that, according to Medtner, must be the beacon of Russian Symbolism. He wrote the book to rescue both Bely and himself, and ultimately to save Russia as well. Through an extensive battery of quotations, he sought to prove that Steiner had willfully misinterpreted and diminished the writer by setting Goethe's speculations on nature in the center of his philosophy when in reality it was on the periphery.

In February 1913, the Anthroposophical Society held its first plenary meeting in Berlin, with Bely and Asya Turgeneva in enthusiastic attendance. In late May to early June that year, Steiner delivered a lecture in Helsingfors on "The Esoteric Significance of the Bhagavad Gita," which was attended by a large group of Russians, all of them associated with the Symbolists, some of them active poets. Now Berdyaev finally had a chance to meet Steiner personally. He and Bely shared a compartment on the train to Helsingfors. Ellis was one of few absent, for he was already moving away from Anthroposophy and toward Catholicism. As in Helsinki the previous year, Steiner held a special talk addressed to the many Russians present in which he explained that only Anthroposophy could "heal" the young soul of the Russian people and help it fulfill its mission on the boundary between East and West. Berdyaev listened with interest, but he remained as ambivalent as ever. On the way home from Helsingfors, Bely met with Blok, Merezhkovsky, and Remizov. He attempted to win them over to Anthroposophy, but met with unanimous dismissal. He encountered another disappointment when he paid a visit outside Moscow to Sergey Solovyov (now his brother-in-law), who had found his place in the Orthodox Church and much like Bulgakov warned against Steiner's "Germanness."

Yet what Bely found so appealing in Steiner's doctrine was precisely its "German" emphasis on the cerebral element in clairvoyance, and its ambition, in defiance of Medtner's warnings, to live up to the demands of Kantianism. At the same time, the skeptical attitudes of his friends seemed the whole time only to aggravate his overwrought state. At one point—in 1908—he had dismissed Steiner as a boring German schoolmaster. Now he decided that his impressions of Steiner's October 1913 lecture series in Norway on Christ would determine whether he would once and for all put his life in the hands of the

Andrey Bely, 1912.

"Master." It is in this light that his apocalyptic reaction to Steiner's appearances in Christiania and Bergen must be viewed. It was here that he thought he had found the Answer, and at that moment it was as though he himself had been transformed into the Russian Christ.

Now Bely broke almost completely both with Medtner, who was giving the final touches to *Reflections on Goethe*, and with Ellis, who had just defected and was in the process of mounting a general attack against his former Master in *Vigilemus!*, which would soon be published by Musagetes with Medtner's consent. In his pamphlet the recently converted Catholic dismissed Steiner as an esoteric sorcerer in rebellion against the Church.

Bely's ecstasy gave way to confusion and desperation. Suddenly, his association with Steiner appeared to have cost him almost all his friends: Medtner, Ellis, Blok, Bulgakov, Merezhkovsky, and Sergey Solovyov. And Russia was far away. In *Petersburg* his inner struggle had found artistic expression. Now that the novel was finished and he had settled into a stationary life in the Anthroposophical commune in Dornach, however, his problems only multiplied as the world war approached. He got some support from Maksimilian Voloshin, who also was in Dornach and was helping build the Anthroposophist sanctuary.

Medtner and Ellis, who were both in Swiss exile not far from the Anthroposophists in Dornach, regarded spiritual science as an attack on true European culture. Back in Russia and surrounded during the war by a number of newly converted occultists, Berdyaev in the December 1916 issue of the journal *Russkaya mysl* (*Russian Thought*), discussed "types of religious thought in Russia," particularly Anthroposophy and Russian religious sectarianism. Attempting to fathom why Russians were so strongly attracted to Steiner's cosmogony and his path of knowledge, he states that especially the apocalyptic temperament of "the Russian Anthroposophists" sets them fundamentally apart from their West European counterparts. It is here that the distance between the Russians and Steiner is greatest. Anthroposophy posits a spiritual evolution through several incarnations, which makes the self servilely dependent upon cosmic processes spanning millennia. Thus there is no instantaneous miracle of reconciliation, such as the mystery that occurred when Christ promised the Good Thief on the cross entry to the Kingdom of God. There is indeed a profound truth in what Steiner teaches about the immanent activity of the Christ impulse in us, but Christ remains all too clearly in the midst of the created world process and is reduced to a mere cosmic agent.

Anthroposophy returns our gaze toward the mysteries of cosmic life, Berdyaev emphasizes. The historic moment has come when we must enter once again upon the path of spiritual knowledge, but we must not become a passive implement of a cosmic process whose meaning is alien to us. Instead it is our task to become co-creators of the new reality. Anthroposophy, unfortunately, is too authoritarian and demands too much obedience of its disciples. Popular Anthroposophical pamphlets sometimes resemble Social Democratic brochures—"party" literature written for propagandistic purposes. Because spiritual scientists must tame their passions, they find it difficult to participate in the spiritual life of their people and risk becoming vaguely neutral. In reality, Berdyaev maintains, it is the eternal "femininity" of the Russian soul that can be sensed in Steiner's popularity in Moscow and

Petersburg. Russian intellectuals always tend to look for masculine organizers of the soul in the West, especially in Germany, because the Russian Logos does not penetrate into the chaos of the Russian soul. The organizing, disciplining principle must always be sought somewhere far away through transcendence. Thus Anthroposophy represents "Westernism" no less than, for example, Marxism. The genuinely Russian Andrey Bely is an especially clear example. He is the greatest creative talent among Steiner's followers. Steinerism can scarcely be said to be felicitous for artistic creativity, but in that respect Bely, who has found important creative impulses in Anthroposophy, has proved to be an exception.

Andrey Bely, 1916.

To us today, Berdyaev's parallels between occultism and Bolshevism and Steiner and Marx may seem odd. They must be viewed in the proper perspective, however, for they indicate how seriously he took Anthroposophy. Russia was on the threshold of enormous upheavals, and it seemed to Berdyaev that Steiner and Marx were in almost equal measure laying claim to the right to interpret and guide the fate of the nation. Significantly enough, a little less than a week before the October revolution, Berdyaev delivered a lecture in Moscow on *Petersburg* in which he portrayed Bely's novel as a brilliant harbinger of the "cosmic whirlwind" that seemed to be sweeping over Russia. Three months later Blok wrote *The Twelve*, in which Christ leads twelve Petrograd revolutionaries through an apocalyptic storm and blizzard. Blok declared that at that moment he heard the roar of history "both within and around" him, adding in his notebooks: "Can Steiner 'control' this roar?" It is telling that it is here—albeit ironically—that he asks the question, for it can be viewed as being addressed to Bely, who had returned to Russia in 1916. Bely would not have hesitated to answer, for at the time he was hectically working among Russian Anthroposophists and cultural workers to fulfill what he regarded as his mission to steer the revolutionary process into spiritual scientific channels.

Around the turn of the year 1916-1917, Bely's rebuttal to Medtner came out, published by the Anthroposophical publishing house Dukhovnoe znanie (Spiritual Knowledge). Verbosely entitled *Rudolf Steiner and Goethe in the Contemporary World View*, it claimed that in his book on Goethe, Medtner had sought to freeze the first verdant shoots of Steiner's revolutionary ideas. He had produced "drawing-room witticisms" at the expense of Anthroposophy, was guilty of willful misinterpretations and contradictions, and had not even bothered to delve into Steiner's collected works on Goethe. Medtner demonstrated that he himself had never fully understood Goethe, for it was in fact Steiner who showed how Goethe's color theory could solve the Kantian problem, emancipate thought, and spiritualize cognition. Medtner's gnoseological limitations created a labyrinth of Knossos with a Minotaur monster at its center. There, Bely tells us, he became hopelessly lost.

Medtner had lived for Goethe and Kant and taken it as his mission to inject Goethean artistic maturity and Kantian intellectual acuity into Russian Symbolism. Now he was being told that he was an amateur. He once again underwent psychotherapy (with none other than Carl Gustav Jung) and eventually responded in the form of a German pamphlet written in Zurich, in which he scrutinized Anthroposophy's "intuitive" path to knowledge and openly mocked Steiner. He lost some of his best friends when two irreconcilable camps formed around him and Bely. Ivan Ilyin and Ellis were his followers until the latter also deserted him because of his profound objections to Medtner's new Jungian outlook.

Over the course of some ten years, virtually all the Symbolists were forced to take up a position on Rudolf Steiner. The 1910s in Russian intellectual life were colored by Anthroposophy.

Bely's Encounter with Rudolf Steiner

*A*ndrey Bely led a nomadic life as he worked on *Petersburg*, his novel about Nikolay, the rebellious son of Senator Ableukhov. Abounding in rhythmicized and richly orchestrated language and imaginative fantasy, the work is intricate to begin with, and this complexity was surely increased even further by the fact that the book was written in 20 different places in five different countries, from October 1911 near Moscow to December 1913 in Berlin. Bely's schedule constantly broke down. At first he thought he would have the novel done in a few months; then July 1912 became the new deadline. At that time, inspired by his first meeting with Rudolf Steiner in May of that year, he was to have finished the book and begin occult training in the theosophical colony in Munich.

As it turned out, however, Bely's encounter with Steiner and the meditation exercises it inspired generated unexpected material for the novel that accounted for much of its true originality and expanded it far beyond its intended scope. The book quite simply became inseparable from Bely's life at the Theosophical colony. Such is the reality behind Bely's 500-page elucidation of the 1905 Revolution.

While at Steiner's colony, Bely delved deeper and deeper into his hero's trauma. Ableukhov Jr. has suppressed his promise to the terrorists to assassinate his father. Now it comes to the surface, and he suddenly acts out his sadistic fantasies. He is deeply ambivalent: on the one hand, he loves his powerful father, who seems to rule over Russia, yet at the same time he hates the idiosyncrasy, extreme cerebralism, shame, and confused sexuality that he has inherited from him. The psychic boundaries between father and son are diffuse. Nikolay feels that he must sever the tie and free himself of the burden of his father. It is as though there is not enough room for them both in physical space.

A 50-page portrait of Bely's father in *On the Border of Two Centuries*, the first part of his memoirs, shows how closely his own psychic problems resembled those of Nikolay Ableukhov. The various genres in Bely's oeuvre constantly interact. His memoirs have unmistakably been influenced by *Petersburg*, while they in turn clearly demonstrate that his attempt to come to terms with his father, Professor of Mathematics Nikolay Bugaev, was a driving force behind his entire oeuvre. Bely was repelled by his father's philosophical positivism and political conservatism, yet strongly bonded to and identifying with him. His trauma came to a climax in the Oedipal drama in the novel and would be followed by several more works with a similar theme. What is remarkable is that he was able to elevate his private predicament to the level of a testimony to the experience of an entire generation.

Bely's drawing of Nikolay Ableukhov in *Petersburg*.

The novel that was already supposed to be finished would occupy Bely for another year and a half as he followed his "Master's" lecture tour around Europe on a kind of "Steineriad." Shortly after completing the work, in February 1914 Bely established himself in the new Anthroposophical commune under construction in Dornach, Switzerland, and thus began a new period in his life and works. He soon entered a crisis, not only because of the outbreak of WWI, but also because *Petersburg* was no longer with him, and the stationary life near Steiner was paralyzing him. Eventually his successful attempts to escape to other places in Switzerland resulted in *Kotik Letaev*, a novel that also drew much valuable material from his experiences at Dornach.

In early October 1912, Bely and Asya Turgeneva settled down in the Swiss spa Vitznau on the north shore of Lake Lucerne, not far from the city of Lucerne. Here he spent three weeks developing chapter six of the novel, material he had begun a year earlier in Bobrovka outside Moscow, and made it the center of the work. This was immediately after he had attended and been deeply impressed by Steiner's series of lectures in Basel entitled "The Gospel According to St. Mark." He meditated morning, noon, and night. This training in "spiritual science," his lively absorption in Steiner's cosmogony, and his personal relationship with the "Master" provided an exceptional stimulus to his writing. He notified the journal *Trudy i dni* from Vitznau that he could no longer serve as Emilii Medtner's co-editor. Bely was rebelling against Medtner in Steiner's name, but he was also motivated by a desire to concentrate all his energy on the novel, which now had found new life.

The depictions of supernatural worlds in Steiner's Theosophy (which toward the end of the year would become Anthroposophy) gave the text a new dimension as in dreams and visions the heroes established contact with the astral cosmos and expanded their personalities out into infinity. Bely achieved striking comic effects with all this, poking fun in the novel things that he held most sacred privately, not least the cherished messianic fantasies of Anthroposophy. He had always proceeded in this manner, with his prose serving as a disarming corrective to his overwrought visions. Most important and artistically most fruitful was his personal filial relationship with Steiner. Practically every encounter with Steiner's dynamic performances behind the lectern became a psychodrama that generated devastating satire in the novel.

At the Hotel Rigibahn (which today is called the Hobby Hotel Terrasse) in Vitznau Bely sank into meditative trances, as prescribed by Steiner, from which he drew directly what would become the expressionistic climax of *Petersburg*. It is impossible to determine exactly how much he had written thus far. Reportedly, there were text fragments that reflected his anxiety in the fall of 1911 as he sat writing in a borrowed house in Bobrovka under paintings of old ancestors who seemed to come to life and step out of their portraits. It is certain, however, that it was merely fragments that he now developed and deepened satirically.

The view from Bely's hotel window in Vitznau. Photo: Martin Ryf.

Here, Bely transfers the events of the novel to unconscious planes, to nightmares and hallucinations, and thus also to the unreality of the Petersburg islands, detached as they are from the Ableukhovs' mainland, which symbolize this dimension. In the center is no longer Nikolay Ableukhov but his "island self," his hidden identity, the "stranger" with the bomb who appears in the first chapter and now steps forward under his real name, Aleksandr Dudkin. What is being described against the backdrop of Petersburg's terrible fall weather is Dudkin's spiritual delirium. The entire tsarist capital shivers with and within him.

Remarkably, this study of nightmare was created amid the incomparable natural splendor of Switzerland. Bely's window looked out on Lake Lucerne, surrounded on all sides by the Alps. Although there often was in fact a mist hanging over the water in Vitznau, no place could seem farther from the claustrophobic stone wasteland of *Petersburg*, shrouded in the germ-ridden thick fogs from which Nikolay Ableukhov does not escape until the epilogue.

Chapter six is divided into two lengthy nightmarish visions that hark back to and build further on key scenes in nineteenth-century Russian literature. First Dudkin is confronted in the dark stairway to his attic room by the devil himself, a figure of Oriental extraction. His name on the one hand is "Enfranshish," on the other "Shishnarfne," since his shadowy world happens to be a mirror image. Bely may have constructed this "Enfranshish" out of German prefixes and suffixes such as ent-, veran-, -zisch that he struggled with as he read and listened to Steiner and was in general trying to cope with what he found to be an alien linguistic environment. Dudkin and the devil (who is never called the devil) have met earlier in Helsingfors, a city that is evidently associated with "Finnish sorcery." As happened with Ivan Karamazov, the devil uses Dudkin's own repressed nihilistic ideas to harass him, reminding him that in Helsingfors he had called for "healthy barbarism" and the destruction of culture. Here there are allusions to Bely's debate around 1907 with the so-called Mystical Anarchists in Petersburg, who at that time personified his fears that Russian literature and ultimately the entire country were being undermined. Dudkin is told that he had urged openness toward chaos. His call for a new barbarism supposedly culminated in a nightmarish act committed in an interplanetary dimension, which in a waking state he dismisses as the beginning of his "illness."

Andrey Bely and Asya Turgeneva, 1912.

The devil forces his way into the shabby, gloomy garret. He is as vulgarly intimate as Ivan's devil, and like him he is also fixated on stomach cramps and colds, emphasizing that the Petersburg climate "is harmful *to me as well.*" Again like Ivan's devil, he touches not only upon physical infirmities, but appears to be familiar with psychiatry. Dudkin is no less irritated than Ivan over falling for this rubbish and his inability to disbelieve in the devil's existence. At this point (after for a time seeming almost corporeal) the devil appears as a hazy contour: now a moonlit smudge of soot on the window, now, as he himself pictures it, as a microbe out of the fumes of the Petersburg swamp. Ultimately his voice seems to issue from Dudkin's own wheezing. He says he wants to collaborate by admitting the anxiety-ridden revolutionary to the icy astral cosmos of his parallel shadow world, to which he will give him a shadow passport. Like his predecessor, he likes to compare the two worlds and complains that he does not have domiciliary rights on "this side." What Dudkin must do, he declares before he disappears, is to commit yet another "act" in order, it is implied, to be finally initiated into Satanism.

The gap between the devil's pettiness and his disquisitions on the icy expanses of the soul is satirically effective. Even Dostoevsky had not gone quite so far. It works due to Steiner's cosmogony.

Dudkin's first phantom vision is soon succeeded by another in a parodical extrapolation of the final section of Pushkin's poem *The Bronze Horseman*, which like *The Brothers Karamazov* is of fundamental significance in regard to Bely's novel. In Pushkin's poem, Peter the Great's Bronze Horseman statue comes to life and chases his rebellious subject Evgeny, who had dared to shake his fist at Petersburg's builder, through the streets of the city. Evgeny goes mad and perishes. In Bely's work, the Horseman again rides forth into the moonlit night and thunders up the stairs to Dudkin's garret in a scene that borrows and varies some of Pushkin's sound imagery. This time, however, he is not out for revenge, but has a common cause with the penitent bomb thrower. He pours his red-hot bronze into Dudkin's veins to give him the strength to conquer his evil spirit, the terrorist organizer Lippanchenko, a close friend and henchman of the devil, who seems to have hypnotic power over Dudkin.

The revolutionary realizes that he has been forgiven by the creator of modern Russia and founder and lord of the city. At the same time, Peter grows into something larger, assuming a new symbolic function in the novel as the merciless historical Fate that haunts the nocturnal visions of Russia's crushed citizens, a mighty and all-destructive cosmic force. Dudkin addresses him as his new "Master," perhaps—well versed as he is in *Revelation*—taking him to be the resurrected Christ on a white steed. The Horseman is no better than Satanism, however, for he as well pronounces the deadly verdict: "I doom: irrevocably." After his visit there is nothing for Dudkin to do but go mad. His body full of boiling bronze, he stabs his revolutionary tormentor to death. But nothing is gained by that act. Within the walls of Petersburg there is no remedy—it can only be found on the outside, in the religiosity of the Russian people with whom Nikolay Ableukhov identifies himself in the epilogue, when he has escaped the nightmares of the spectral city.

Dudkin has entertained thoughts of being a superman, and his development is reminiscent of Friedrich Nietzsche's. Bely early on became interested in Nietzsche's fate and mental breakdown. Was it disintegration or an act of freedom—a step out into a new dimension? Only Russian intellectuals, Bely believed, could understand Nietzsche, for they were in a life-and-death struggle with his problems. It was in Basel that Nietzsche's psychic crisis had begun; Bely had just spoken about this in Basel with Vyacheslav Ivanov. Nietzsche had described himself as dynamite, which is reflected in *Petersburg* especially in Bely's portrait of Nikolay Ableukhov as the bearer of his own internal bomb. In Oberengadin in southeastern Switzerland, Nietzsche wrote *Thus Spoke Zarathustra*, which plays considerably on correspondences between the human psyche and the alpine landscape. In the beginning of chapter six Dudkin interprets Nikolay Ableukhov's "bomb trances" as the transports of Nietzschean Dionysian mysteries. Like Nietzsche, Dudkin senses the chasm within himself, something that Zarathustra also speaks of when he describes Man as "a rope over an abyss."

The article Bely was writing parallel with this chapter in the novel shows that he was thinking intensively about the German philosopher. "Circular Movement," as it was titled when it appeared in *Trudy i dni*, describes Nietzsche as leaping to his death into the Swiss abyss. His idea of "eternal return" had imprisoned him—and with him modernism as a whole—in a tragic circle in which everything was merely repeated in reverse order and inside out, as in the mirror world represented by the devil in the novel.

It was probably no coincidence that after his stay in Basel Bely decided to settle in Vitznau, at the foot of the famous Rigi massif. As he set out to penetrate the deepest strata of the Russian rebel's personality he perceived a real connection between the two meanings of the German word "Alp": mountain and nightmare. To be able to portray the dark chasms of the Russian soul he needed to be surrounded by the stunningly beautiful crags of Switzerland.

When *Petersburg* was finished a little over a year later and Bely's "Steineriad" was over, he visited Nietzsche's native village and fell to his knees on his grave in almost mystical-apocalyptic exaltation. The ambiguity of Nietzsche's illness probably remained an essentially unresolved problem for him. The pose, imitating the Bronze Horseman, that the insane Dudkin strikes over the bloody corpse of his inner oppressor in the final scene of chapter seven definitely had not pointed to a solution.

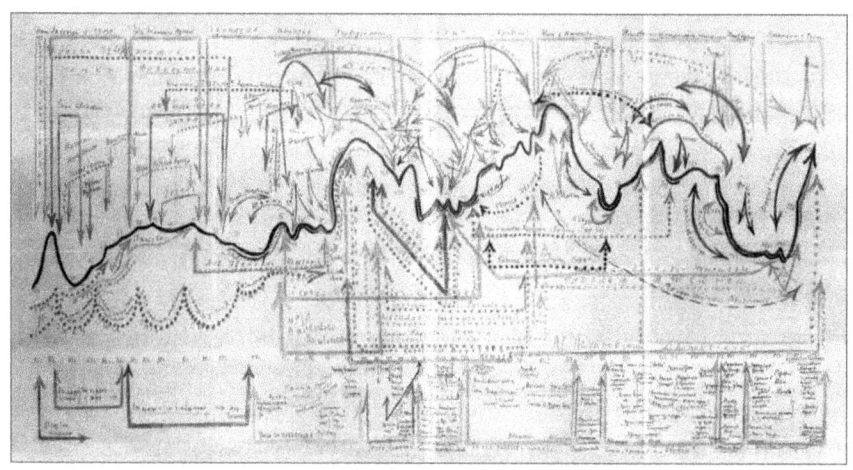

Bely's "Lifeline"—an attempt to summarize his personal and artistic evolution and important influences from his first conscious moments in 1883 at the age of 2-3 up to 1927, when he drew the sketch. (For the bigger image please see pp. 152-153).

Freud's Unknown Russian Patient

In the late spring of 1914 the philosopher Ivan Ilyin underwent seven weeks of intensive therapy with Sigmund Freud in Vienna. It is quite remarkable that thus far no historian of psychoanalysis has noted this strange meeting between such a significant Russian cultural personage and Freud.

At the time he met Freud, Ilyin was a young university lecturer who had studied in Germany. Although successful academically, he struggled with severe personal problems. Dostoevsky once defined the Russian character as "maximalist." No one was more maximalist than Ilyin. He swung between extremes—between rancor and tender sentimentality, aggressiveness and reverie, intense need for human contact and self-imposed isolation and solitude. Politically he had drifted from one opposite to the other. First, in connection with the 1905 Revolution, he severed relations with his father and distanced himself from his aristocratic family, among the oldest in Russia, and became an adherent of Anarchism and Social Democracy. He is even reported to have attended the December 1905 Social Democratic Congress in Tampere, at which Lenin and Stalin first confronted each other. By the time he met Freud, however, the pendulum had swung in the opposite direction. Now he professed a conservative nationalism of a strongly sentimental bent rooted in Orthodoxy. Conservative not only politically but also aesthetically, he was opposed to modernist currents and had proclaimed Symbolism, which he regarded as a dangerous decadent attack on the sacred foundations of being, to be his archenemy.

Ilyin's newly aroused nationalism may have played a compensatory role. He was actually only half-Russian, since his mother was from an immigrant German family. Thus, behind his political changeovers there was in fact a dual family heritage. On the one hand, his grandfather and namesake held the heavily symbolic post of keeper of the Kremlin gates. His father (who became a lawyer) had been born in the Kremlin, and was not only named after Tsar Alexander II but was reportedly even his godson. On the other hand, in the "progressive" 1860s, one of his paternal aunts had responded to her strict conservative upbringing by fleeing from the Kremlin and marrying into a noted extended socialist family in Petersburg, about whom she later wrote a well-known memoir. Another paternal aunt married the progressive Jewish pedagogue Yakov Gurevich, who headed his own secondary school in Petersburg and passed on his liberal views to his daughter Lyubov Gurevich, one of Russia's most prominent journalists and the editor of the periodical *Severny vestnik* (*The Northern Messenger*). Seventeen years Ilyin's senior, she became especially close to him. Thus the tension between Moscow Slavophilism and Petersburg liberalism, and that between monarchism and nascent revolutionary notions, was present already in his family background.

Ilyin probably discovered Freud around 1909, the year that psychoanalysis had its first early breakthrough in Moscow. It was at this time that he read Otto Weininger's *Sex and Character*, which abounds in references to deep psychology. In early 1911, he studied with Georg Simmel in Berlin, where he wrote an essay in the spirit of Simmel's philosophy of culture entitled "On Civility"—which was perhaps what came hardest to him—in which he refers in a note to Freud as "a profound and subtle psychologist." During these years he gravitated more or less exclusively to Jewish authorities such as Simmel, Husserl, and Freud. In Berlin as well he kept almost entirely to a circle of Russian Jewish students. It is possible to conclude that this predilection was derived largely from the ease with which he adapted to the Gurevichs as his "alternative family" in Petersburg.

Home in Russia after long sojourns at German universities, in the spring of 1913 Ilyin became acquainted with the composer Nikolay Medtner and his brother Emilii. Nikolay Medtner's music, which tended toward the classical at a time when almost everything was subversively avant-gardist, seemed to embody his own ideals. Nikolay was easy-going, whereas Emilii was a combative, militant anti-modernist who in his criticism portrayed the new music, represented by composers influenced by esotericism such as Aleksandr Scriabin, as a frontal assault on European culture self-evidently centered in Germany. A profound double friendship developed between the Medtner brothers and Ilyin. Emilii had just published his manifesto *Modernism and Music*, which Ilyin enthusiastically welcomed, for it was very much in line with his own new rigidly conservative aesthetic values. He was willing to overlook the fact that the book portrayed modernism as a Jewish conspiracy, but it was a little more difficult for him to accept Medtner's disparagement of Russian culture. Both men were German-Russians, but they differed in their attitudes toward their backgrounds.

Ilyin soon came to Medtner's support and assisted him in his work on *Reflections on Goethe*, through which Medtner attempted to rescue his friend Bely—and ultimately all of Russia—from Rudolf Steiner's "false" claims to Goethe. Ilyin was himself working on a master's thesis on Hegel, so each had his German "research topic." When Medtner's conflict with Bely worsened and his suffering intensified, Ilyin began to recommend that he visit Freud in Vienna. What Medtner told him about his friend Bely's "treachery" and Anthroposophical "aberrations" evidently made his own bilious rejection of Symbolism even more categorical.

By this point in 1913, Freud's works were quite well known in Russia. Ilyin was planning his own pilgrimage to Vienna and probably sent Medtner there on reconnaissance. In October 1913, Medtner contacted Freud in Vienna for a consultation. His positive report home to Ilyin obviously did not fail to produce the desired effect, and in May 1914 Ilyin set off for Vienna for a seven-week course of therapy. His first account in the form of a postcard to Medtner was unreservedly positive. He declared that he had "rather liked our high priest" from the very start. Ilyin was not as generous as his friend when it came to revealing the content of his therapeutic conversations. All we know is that the sessions with Freud were valuable and that they seem to have helped him write his dissertation on Hegel.

Significantly enough, Ilyin's therapy partly coincided with the final phase of Freud's treatment of the "Wolfman," Sergey Pankeev. Freud points out in his case study that it was in this final stage that everything fell into place in Pankeev's therapy and he managed to uncover his patient's "primal trauma." One wonders whether Ilyin's treatment might not have provided some illuminating insights. Ilyin and Pankeev belonged to the same generation of Russian intelligentsia, and they had the same vivid memories of 1905. As has been noted elsewhere, Ilyin seemed to be a character straight out of one of Dostoevsky's novels. Andrey Bely, for example, compared him to Nikolay Stavrogin in *The Possessed*. Even more appropriate, perhaps, are the four Karamazov brothers. He seemed to possess traits of all of them: the hyperintellectual Ivan, the pious Alyosha, the violently emotional Mitya, and the infernal Smerdyakov. Considering the fierce falling out he had with his father in 1905, he may well have lent something to Nikolay Ableukhov in *Petersburg*.

As he was beginning his work on Dostoevsky, Freud probably had both Pankeev and Ilyin in mind when, in an often quoted 1920 letter to Stefan Zweig, he characterized emotional dualism, or the ability to embrace opposite emotional states and push them to an extreme, as archetypically Russian. Perhaps this study should be linked not only to Pankeev, as it has been already, but also to Freud's experiences with Ilyin. Freud highlights the masochistic and latent homosexual traits in Dostoevsky's personality as reflected in his protagonists. Similar tendencies would seem to underlie Ilyin's difficulties and psychic swings. Just like Dostoevsky, Ilyin was a revolutionary who switched sides and went from socialist rebellion to monarchism and nationalism.

In a lecture delivered to a circle of Moscow philosophy students, the first autumn of the war in 1914 Ilyin spoke of the need for the artistic intelligentsia to process "all the wounds in the tissue of the soul that have marked us since childhood, that live on unhealed throughout our lives and gnaw at the soul, rendering many of us victims of neurasthenia and all manner of morbid perversions." He went on, with profound emotion, to address child battering, perhaps on the basis of his own experience. Freud had brought him to insight but had hardly healed his wounds, and his irritable aggressiveness had not diminished. In the fall of 1914 he became closer friends with Nikolay Medtner, who was suffering from depression. He had lost Emilii's day-to-day support, since they were now separated by the war. Like Emilii, Nikolay reacted to the war between Russia and Germany as a personal trauma. He was afflicted with apathy and creative impotence, and there was even talk of Ilyin psychoanalyzing him on his own.

During these months after returning from Vienna, Ilyin was obsessed with psychoanalysis, diagnosing everything and everyone in Freudian terms, reducing every personal problem to neurotic symptoms, and according to one observer, psychoanalyzing every little gesture of those around him. His negative attitude to Symbolism reached the boiling point after Emilii Medtner's near breakdown in the wake of Bely's conversion to Anthroposophy. Ilyin believed that he could use Freud's tools to penetrate the minds of the leading Symbolist figures. He apparently suspected several of them to be latent homosexuals. Perhaps, he recognized in them traits of his own of which he had become aware and was attempting to address. He was married to a philosopher colleague, Natalya, but at the same time had become involved in a few infatuated friendships with men. This might explain his documented, mysterious extreme aversion toward the Symbolist writers as a form of projection or struggle with his own demons.

Ivan Ilyin, 1916.

Now that Bely had fled to Anthroposophy and was no longer in the picture, Vyacheslav Ivanov, who had recently moved to Moscow from Petersburg, became Ilyin's bête noire. Ivanov was a classical scholar, trained in philosophy, and deeply interested in music, which made him Ilyin's rival in his own fields. He had a Dionysian personality, and in fact his entire Symbolist doctrine was based on the cult of Dionysus. He had earlier attempted to conduct a couple of bisexual cohabitation experiments, and had moreover come close to violating the incest taboo when he remarried with his stepdaughter a few years after his wife's death. All this must have made him seem particularly provocative to Ilyin—here was a self-assertive double whose lack of inhibition called into question and undermined both his ideological foundations and his superego defenses. This was a frequent pattern in Russia's thoroughly boundary-transcendent culture around the turn of the century, where personality, politics, and ideology became tightly intertwined in friendships and conflicts.

When in the fall of 1914 religious philosophers, headed by Vyacheslav Ivanov, enunciated their view of the war at the Religious-Philosophical Society in Moscow, Ilyin was pointedly absent. Shortly thereafter, he delivered his own patriotic lecture on "The Spiritual Significance of the War." It came out a few months later in book form, dedicated to Nikolay Medtner, who had now become his supreme cult figure. His antagonistic doppelganger relationship with Ivanov was thereby only reinforced, for Ivanov had at this time established close personal ties to the increasingly extravagant modernist composer Scriabin, who with Sergey Rakhmaninov was Nikolay's chief rival on the Russian concert stage. Ivanov's poetry had made a strong impression on Scriabin, who in November 1914 read aloud to him the text of "Preliminary Act," the prelude to a grandiose musical temple rite he was planning. Ivanov enthusiastically supported him in this somewhat megalomaniacal occult-theurgic project, by which Scriabin hoped to help lead Russia into a new spiritual dimension. Then Scriabin died suddenly in April 1915. Ivanov wrote two sonnets to his memory.

In the fall of 1915, Ivanov wrote "Scriabin's View of Art," a lecture he delivered in December. At this point something happened that, as far as Ilyin was concerned, was not supposed to happen. Deprived of the object of his cult, Ivanov began to gravitate toward Nikolay Medtner. In early November, Sergey Kusevitsky performed a memorial concert for Scriabin in Moscow. The program included *Poème de l'Extase* and *Prometheus*. During the intermission, Ilyin saw Ivanov, at a distance, go up to Nikolay Medtner and inquire about paying him a visit (and hinting at possible collaboration). Ilyin was furious. The "double" was attempting to crowd him out and "conquer" the malleable, passive Nikolay and put him in Scriabin's place for his own ulterior motives. He had already been vexed by the fact that the prominent conductor Kusevitsky, who had now once again taken up Scriabin's music after a much noted break with it a few years earlier, had begun associating with Nikolay. All this was too much for Ilyin.

As early as 1912, Ilyin had admitted to Lyubov Gurevich that his interests were divided between Stanislavsky's "studio," where he even hoped to become an "idea consultant," and the psychiatric clinic, that is, between the theater and therapy. Bely reports that Ilyin sometimes would stand behind Ivanov, mimicking and caricaturing his gestures and openly posing as a double. Here he seems to have been combining his two extremes, both playing theater and enacting his "diagnosis" of Ivanov. Now he took this game one step further, writing a letter to Nikolay Medtner in Ivanov's name, in which he produced a sophisticated parody of the poet's archaizing language and at the same time made sexual innuendos in an attempt to expose his rival's hidden pretensions.

Vyacheslav Ivanov, 1913.

The letter turned out to be a successful practical joke. Nikolay took it quite seriously and very much to heart. He found it to be "unnecessarily bombastic" and at the same time "somewhat derisive." He decided to go to Ivanov and tell him frankly how different and essentially alien they were to each other. He did not get that far, however, because Ilyin forestalled him and revealed the ruse in time. After this incident Ivanov made no further efforts to get closer to Nikolay.

After the letter Ilyin appeared to be through with Ivanov. Now he was waiting to settle accounts with Bely on behalf of both himself and Emilii Medtner. It took a while, but the time came. After Bely's frontal attack on Medtner in *Rudolf Steiner and Goethe in the Contemporary World View*, Ilyin focused all his animosity on Bely. In mid-February 1917, just before the Revolution and the overthrow of the tsar, he stood up in defense of his cherished friend in an extremely aggressive open letter to Bely in which the assault on Medtner was interpreted as a disease symptom, evidence of the degeneration and decay permeating the new literature. In early March, just as the monarchy fell, another open letter with the same message was sent to philosopher Prince Evgeny Trubetskoy. Ilyin obviously considered literature responsible for the Revolution, so there was some logic in his raging diatribes. When the second, Bolshevik upheaval occurred in the fall, he seemed to have regarded it to an even higher degree as a consequence of the Symbolists' moral dissolution. Andrey Bely and Aleksandr Blok were among the first writers to greet the new order in their poetry.

After the October revolution, Ilyin became active as an anti-Soviet professor of philosophy and was arrested several times. Together with some psychiatrists and others, in 1921 he started a psychoanalytical society, dedicated primarily to researching the conditions of "creation," that partly helped to lay the foundation for several years of intensive Freudian activity in the new Soviet state. A year later, with a collective death penalty hanging over them, he and some 200 leading intellectuals and academics in various fields, among them representatives of idealist, non-materialist philosophy, were thrown out of Russia. In exile in Berlin he again metamorphosed, setting aside philosophy and dedicating himself body and soul to the anti-Soviet struggle. From his base in Berlin he wrote books and countless articles and traveled tirelessly around Europe delivering hundreds of lectures on the poison of Bolshevism and Russia's imminent doom.

Ilyin never again uttered a single word about either his socialist or psychoanalytical past. He would inevitably throw in his lot with Fascism. He was an early admirer of Mussolini, and in 1932 he wrote about Germany's immediate need of a "Führer." On the occasion of the "Machtübernahme" in 1933, he sent a personal congratulatory telegram to Hitler and initiated collaboration with

Goebbels' Ministry of Propaganda. The old maximalist was true to form: from a Judeophile he had become a kind of anti-Semitic agitator who denounced "Jewish Bolsheviks" in his writings. However, he eventually found it extremely difficult to cooperate with the Nazis. In 1938, after being interrogated by Alfred Rosenberg's right-hand man, he was for the second time thrown out of a totalitarian country. His old friend Sergey Rakhmaninov helped him get to Switzerland. He settled down in Zurich, where he had once visited Emilii Medtner and even lectured at Jung's Psychological Club.

*Ivan Ilyin as **The Thinker** by Mikhail Nesterov, 1921-1922.*

Ilyin lived until 1954. He sometimes proclaimed that his only real concern was Russia. As he himself put it, he was forever a child in Mother Russia's arms. One gets the feeling that his sharp intellect was nearly powerless in the face of his infantile inhibitions.

Emilii Medtner
and Carl Gustav Jung

The highly charged friendship between Emilii Medtner and Andrey Bely dates to the early 1900s. Of German descent on both sides of his family, Medtner had a strong, controlling personality and took it upon himself to steer Bely's modernist experiments and visionary raptures toward German culture. And Bely went along. Deep down, Emilii had serious personal problems, including an unnatural bond to his brother, the composer Nikolay Medtner, whom he tried to push in the same direction (and who soon would come to share his wife).

In the wake of the 1905 Revolution, Medtner resigned from his post in the state censorship and began a new career as a critic and freelance musico-philosophical journalist. With music and philosophy as his two overarching interests, he aspired to linking Russia closer to Germany and guiding the entire Symbolist movement into Germanic channels.

In 1909 Medtner took a definitive step toward fulfilling his mission when he founded the Musagetes publishing house, where, with the god of the Muses, Apollo, as his inspiration, he intended to tame the Dionysian strain in the new art and gather the Symbolist writers around Bely. Bely's creative genius would become the "watchword and banner" of the publishing venture. Germany would help to "heal" Russia. Turgid Russian modernism would be reshaped on the model of Kant and Goethe.

Thus it came as a deep shock to Medtner when Bely decided to join Rudolf Steiner's Theosophical-Anthroposophical colony in Germany and gradually withdrew from Musagetes. Medtner regarded Steiner as both a dangerous rival and an inarticulate preacher whose "hodge-podge of quasi-religions" threatened to emasculate Bely artistically. In his view, Steiner had a very limited knowledge of Kant's philosophy and even less of Goethe's.

In 1912 Musagetes published *Modernism and Music*, a collection of Medtner's articles in which modernism was more or less defined as a Jewish conspiracy. Medtner had early on assimilated aggressive racist ideas, subscribing to Houston Stewart Chamberlain's view of European culture as a struggle between subversive Semitic and constructive German-Aryan forces. Shaken and tormented by Bely's defection, he was also soon working on *Reflections on Goethe* as a form of personal therapy in which he fiercely called into question Anthroposophy's interpretation of Goethe.

Emilii Medtner on the right, with his brother Nikolay and wife Anna in Nizhny Novgorod, 1904.

Under these circumstances Medtner began suffering from recurrent nightmares and shifting psychosomatic symptoms. It was as though a war was being fought deep within him. A desperate reconciliatory meeting with Bely arranged in Munich by Marietta Shaginyan came to nothing. Shortly thereafter, encouraged by his friend Ivan Ilyin, Medtner went in October 1912 to Vienna to consult with Freud. He reportedly told Freud about a very disturbing dream he had had that summer of violent sibling rivalry (a sister tried to strangle another sister, who was perhaps actually himself). He supposedly went on to describe the anxiety he had experienced since childhood, the psychic basis of which he now began to discern. Freud is said to have interpreted this "pseudo-Ménière's disease" of his as the unresolved birth pangs of his personality and urged him to take the initiative and "get married" — there were several possible candidates — and "not to despair," since there was a cure. Finally,

Emilii Medtner, circa 1910.

Freud suggested that he return for intensive therapy the following summer, when he would be free from his publishing duties.

The primary targets of Medtner's attacks in *Reflections on Goethe* are Steiner's alleged underestimation of Kant's role in Goethe's life and his overestimation of Goethe's philosophy of nature. He maintains that Steiner emphasizes and praises Goethe's limitations at the same time that he diminishes and trivializes the real manifestations of his greatness. According to Medtner, Goethe's crucial meeting with Schiller infused his thought with Kantian criticism. It was a vaccine that saved him at a stage when he risked being led astray by his empathy with nature. Steiner, Medtner goes on, misinterprets this encounter when he says that Goethe resisted Kant, when in fact it was Kantian insight that gave the mature Goethe a foundation on which to stand.

Furthermore, Medtner declares, there is a naïve innocence in Goethe's nature philosophy and speculations on a "protoplant" and "protophenomenon" that Steiner fails to perceive. Steiner fails to take into account the lyrical stamp of Goethe's writings on such matters. The fact is, at the turn of the century it was from Goethe that Steiner had drawn the strength to manifest his experience of the reality of the world beyond. It was with the support of Goethe's nature philosophy that Steiner attempted to discover the basis of spiritual clairvoyance in meditation and assert its compatibility with the scientific method. In Medtner's opinion, Steiner had gotten the emphases in Goethe all wrong.

Medtner finished *Reflections on Goethe* in the spring of 1914. Tormented by panic attacks, anxiety, and suicidal thoughts, he was soon feeling even worse. It was in such a state that he read the newly

Emilii Medtner and Carl Gustav Jung

Andrey Bely on a visit to the Medtners in 1911. From the left: Emilii, Nikolay, Anna, Bely, and pianist Nikolay Stember, Nikolay's pupil and second cousin.

published final chapters of *Petersburg*, to which he reacted with a spontaneous outburst in a letter to Bely: "Gasping (to the point of debility): something unbearable, you want to shout: It can't be like this! Stop!!! Help, it's robbery! The human being has been stolen, removed, leaving only his underwear! At the same time, even your enemies must admit that no one else in the world today is capable of writing anything comparable (with respect to portraying our deepest layers)." It seems that Medtner was staring into himself as he read Bely's phantasmal novel. Never, as he put it himself, had his soul felt more repulsive than in these, the most extreme of times.

When Medtner returned to Vienna in July 1914, Freud was on vacation. And then the war broke out. According to his own account, Medtner received the news during an intermission at a Wagner opera in Munich. His only response was panic—it was as though the war activated his own problem, the tension within him between German and Russian. All of his dreams had been dashed. His personal conflict suddenly seemed to lie out in the open on the European battlefield. It was under such circumstances that he made his way to neutral Switzerland to consult with Carl Gustav Jung in Zurich, with whom he soon was undergoing therapy five days a week. When *Reflections on Goethe*, delayed by a printers' strike, appeared in the early fall, it passed almost without a trace. Its message—that Russian culture must look to Germany for leadership—sounded at that particular moment almost like treason.

Medtner's therapy sessions with Jung turned out well for both of them. Jung was himself going through a serious crisis after his painful break with Freud, and he and Medtner seem to have sensed a deep kinship from the start. Medtner sent detailed reports on the progress of the analysis to his wife in Russia. He was inclined to view Jung as a genuine Symbolist. He read his major study of myth *Symbols of Transformation*, and Jung delved into a German translation of Bely's *The Silver Dove*. Medtner found Jung to be perhaps more artist than psychiatrist, while for his part Jung pronounced Medtner "the most modern man" he had ever met. In Medtner's inner split he perceived "the increasingly critical relationship between rational and irrational in the contemporary man of culture." He was fascinated not least by Medtner's "mythical thinking," which he perceived to be something "suprapersonal" and "medial" in his psyche. Jung recounts in his fragmentary reminiscences that he was convinced by his own crisis and tumultuous inner imagery during the first months of the war that he himself belonged to all humanity and was expressing a collective unconscious. He interpreted Medtner's inner drama and anxiety dreams in the same way. He believed that the cataclysm of war had been anticipated by certain especially sensitive personalities.

What Medtner reported in letters, of course, should be approached with caution, yet it must be said that there probably was a grain of truth in his feeling that, during this period, Jung came to relate to him with something like love. Medtner afforded the therapist access to the entire Symbolist experience at a stage where Jung was for the first time standing on his own two feet and was in the process of articulating his own psychological theories. Medtner describes the relationship as follows in one of his letters:

One general rule is what is known as *Übertragung* [transference; M.L.], (quite simply a form of falling in love) toward the psychoanalyst, but since I am an "old coquette," the opposite has occurred. I like Jung, he is an admirable European, one of the most learned and cultured individuals I've met and very amiable besides. . . . But with me there is no question of *Übertragung*. . . . It is Jung who has übertragt to me to such an extent that I think I hear Ilyin—or one of the others who are in love with me. . . . He regards me as a *verkümmertes Genie* [stunted genius; M.L.] and is constantly amazed by the power of my thought. . . . He perceives something particularly prophetic in my personality. He told me the other day that eyes like mine can only be found on the canvases of the *Trecentists* (i.e. the pre-Raphaelites, Botticelli, Filippo Lippi, Francesco Francia); you see how far things have gone! On the surface as well. His assessment of my inner self is in the same vein!

Medtner later wrote that he and his therapist were struck by the remarkable coincidences in their backgrounds. Both had been strongly influenced early on by their reading of Goethe and Nietzsche. At the same time that Jung was publishing his study on myth, Medtner was working on Goethe and the symbolism of Faust in his polemic with Anthroposophy, where he had attempted to show how Goethe successfully dealt with his "midlife crisis" in the 1790s, when his "spirit" had risked perdition by descending into the dark maternal cave of "nature" but had returned healed and reborn. He spoke of the sun as Goethe's and Faust's overarching symbol, the light of noon that enveloped the enlightened mature poet. Jung had written about the very same thing in his study when he described the mythical hero dying and being reborn again as he follows the path of the sun.

Jung emphasizes in his memoirs that his entire subsequent production was based on what he went through and developed during these war years when Medtner (with some interruptions) was his patient, and Medtner notes in his commemorative essay on Jung that he recognized their conversations as the raw material in much of what his therapist later wrote, not least with respect to his so-called theory of psychological types.

Ironically enough, Bely had ended up in Dornach, only an hour away from Basel and Medtner, where he was participating in building the Anthroposophists' new "spiritual university," Johannisbau, later renamed Goetheanum. Medtner visited him several times despite their conflict. He had now taken up with Asya Turgeneva's elder sister Natalya, who was a member of the commune. Around Christmas 1914 Bely took him on a tour of the emerging esoteric sanctuary. In letters that Medtner wrote home, he said he felt like Dante being led by Virgil through hell, purgatory, and heaven. The sounds of war could be heard from the French battlefield in the distance. Suddenly they ran into Steiner. According to Medtner, Bely behaved almost hysterically in the presence of his "Master" whereas Steiner was remarkably simple in his manner.

Toward the end of 1914, Bely finally got hold of a copy of Medtner's pamphlet on Steiner. He set to work almost immediately on his response. When Medtner visited him in the spring of 1915 and heard him read some passages from the manuscript, he was so shocked that he fled from Dornach, never to see Bely again. Soon he was immersed in his next major undertaking, which was to get Jung's writings translated into Russian, a project he felt would bring to Russia a new and very specific remedy. Eventually, he engaged a group of exiled Mensheviks in Zurich as translators.

The October coup in Russia almost passed Medtner by. He had completed his analysis relatively successfully in early 1917, although he himself admitted that it was not so easy to transform a "sick devil" into a "healthy angel." Bely had returned home, and in the fall Medtner gained access to his former friend's response to his book on Goethe. Bely's assault on his work and on him personally was so painful that he had to undergo a brief period of intense therapy with Jung to keep from collapsing entirely. The attack was worse than what he had heard and reacted so strongly to in Dornach in 1915. Bely's book claimed that Medtner was an ignorant amateur, whereas Rudolf Steiner was opening up entire new dimensions for modern humanity.

During this difficult time Jung and Medtner drew even closer to each other. According to what he later recalled, Medtner wanted to shout "My friend is dead! Long live my friend!" For the next few years he was Jung's closest and perhaps in reality only friend, who accompanied him on sailing outings and camping and hiking trips in the Alps, spent holidays with Jung and his family, and was even a Sunday dinner guest in their home. Medtner reported in a letter to his wife: "What a remarkable person he is! And how pleasantly profound, humorously mysterious, ursinely masculine.... Especially on excursions one appreciates the breadth of his erudition and his almost encyclopedic knowledge. It is very salutary that Jung is so cheerful despite his dreadful depth and complication."

To Medtner, Jung seemed to be almost a Goethean total personality (a family legend had it that he was also a descendant of Goethe). It was as though he was fulfilling the mission for which Bely had been intended. He had united life and science and become one with his psychology. The Russian Symbolists had similarly attempted to fuse their lives and their art. Just as Bely had done, through his expansiveness and magic Jung appeared to bring everyone around him—family members, relatives, colleagues and friends—into the enchanted circle of his growing movement.

When Jung's "laboratory experiments" from the war years were published in 1921 in his next major work, *Psychological Types*, it went without saying that Medtner would review it. In two installments in *Neue Zürcher Zeitung* he declared that so-called analytical psychology had "laid its confident hand on a problem that has occupied the artist's senses for decades." He thought that Jung's definition of the symbol as a bridge that was neither rational nor irrational between the intellect and emotion was among the best ever formulated on the subject. There was, however, a cautionary undertone in his review that had to do with Jung's growing interest in Gnosticism and various mystical doctrines. A year later this led to open conflict between the two men, since Medtner feared that Jung was losing his foothold in Kant and relying too heavily on "intuition." Their intimate collaboration came to an end, although Medtner remained a Jungian. Although the translation of Jung's works went forward, the Russian texts were heavily edited while the translators had returned via Stockholm to revolutionary Russia with the original texts in their baggage.

In 1923 in Zurich, Medtner published his belated reaction to Bely's response to his book on Goethe in the form of a collection of vehemently polemical essays aimed at Anthroposophy's claims to knowledge and its overconfidence in "intuition." There was a word of warning to Jung as well. Originating from lectures held at the Psychological Club, the volume bore the prolix title *On So Called "Intuition": Notions Adjacent and Problems Related Thereto*.

Medtner and Jung reestablished relations in the mid-1920s. Medtner also began conducting psychoanalysis himself. In 1931, two years after the Russian translation of *Psychological Types* came out under his editorship in Berlin, he delivered a lecture at the Psychological Club in which he attempted to describe Russia in Jungian terms. He explained that the pronounced dualism and constant play of opposites in Russian society had intensified to the level of a "national neurosis." He suggested that because analytical psychology focused on personality polarities, it was especially well suited to bring self-awareness to the Russian nation.

In 1935, Medtner and Toni Wolff edited the Festschrift commemorating Jung's sixtieth birthday. Although Medtner characterized Jung as a living ego ideal in his life, his article in the collection was not entirely honest, for Jung had again begun to slip away from him and had become increasingly interested in alchemy and other such subjects. Medtner did not attend the birthday celebration. A year later, he died in Germany as a dedicated Nazi. An inveterate anti-Semite, he thoroughly approved of the German "Jewish policy." In his deepening bitterness, his only support was Adolf Hitler—this man with the brilliant soul of an artist who became involved in politics in an effort to give a foundering Europe solid Teutonic ground on which to stand. As for Jung, his uncritical attitude at this time toward Nazism, to put it mildly, should definitely also be viewed in the light of Medtner's longstanding political influence on him. Early on, Medtner had attempted to persuade Jung to support Mussolini.

Medtner died at a mental clinic in Dresden, the city to which he had come to witness the German miracle with his own eyes. Paradoxically, although he had wanted to guide Russian Symbolism in the direction of Germany, what in fact happened instead was

Emilii Medtner and Carl Gustav Jung

From the left: psychiatrist Hans Trüb, Emma Jung, Emilii Medtner, Trüb's son Georg, and Jung on an outing to Alp Laui, Toggenburg in 1921.

that he brought something specifically Russian to Germanophone culture in the form of the Symbolist experience. In two different phases, he was close to two great European artistic personalities, so to speak. Bely's and Jung's messages to the world had much in common: if it is not bridged, the split in contemporary humanity—the gap between conscious and unconscious, between the self and others, between intellect and emotion—threatens culture with destruction.

Boris Pasternak and Goethe

In March 1909, nineteen-year-old Boris Pasternak once met his idol Aleksandr Scriabin to show his attempts in musical composition. Despite Scriabin's praise and encouragement, their meeting led Pasternak to the decision to stop pursuing the career of a composer. During that conversation, Skryabin also advised him to abandon his law studies and take up philosophy instead. That fall Pasternak did so, and was soon drawn into the circle around the newly founded Musagetes publishing house.

In his 1956 autobiographical sketch, Pasternak described Musagetes as "something of an academy" in which the leading Moscow Symbolists "and the enthusiastic youth discussed rhythm, the history of German Romanticism, Russian lyrical poetry, Goethe's and Richard Wagner's aesthetics, Baudelaire and the French Symbolists, and ancient Greek pre-Socratic philosophy." He emphasized that Andrey Bely was the "soul" and "authority" in all these endeavors, the same Bely who, now that Pasternak had switched to philosophy and literature, was perhaps taking the place of Scriabin in his life.

Pasternak visited two circles created by Musagetes publishing house – one on history of philosophy led by Fyodor Stepun and the other devoted to "studies of the problems of aesthetic culture and Symbolist art," the so called Young Musagetes, that held forth in Konstantin Krakht's sculpture studio.

In May 1912, Pasternak went to Marburg to study under Hermann Cohen. What brought him there, besides Cohen's highly theoretical solutions to the problem of knowledge, was the Marburg school's broad view of cultural history, which resonated with the interests of the Young Musagetes.

After his return from Germany, Pasternak joined a group of young Musagetes poets. In June of 1913, they brought out together an anthology, *Lyrical Poetry*, within a new publishing house with the same name (Lirika).

In February 1913, Pasternak held a talk at Young Musagetes entitled "Symbolism and Immortality." This was his first attempt to express his aesthetic creed. In it he attributed a universal significance to the artist's extreme subjectivity, maintaining that this is the vehicle through which artists convey their creative inspiration to posterity and thereby become immortal. Subjectivity, it turns out, is supraindividual.

Lirika had a distinctly German profile. Besides a collection of Pasternak's essays entitled *Symbolism and Immortality*, planned publications in the fall of 1913 included translations of Rilke's poetry, an interpretation of Goethe's unfinished poem "The Mysteries," and a translation of Novalis' novel *Heinrich von Ofterdingen* (of these plans, however, only Rilke's *The Book of Hours* and Goethe's poem were actually published). Lirika was undergoing a split caused by the clashes around Anthroposophy. As a result, in early 1914, Pasternak, Sergey Bobrov, and Nikolay Aseev, left Lirika and founded Tsentrifuga (The Centrifuge). Pasternak was faced with a situation in which all of his former authorities and friends seemed to be choosing Theosophy or Anthroposophy. Scriabin and his composition teacher Reinhold Glière were the first, followed, among others, by Bely and Pasternak's close friend of several years, the poet Yulian Anisimov. Pasternak shared Bobrov's skepticism toward esotericism. In May of 1914, Bobrov, Aseev, and Pasternak published a futuristic volume with the strange name *Rukonog* (*Brachiopod*), which was a kind of manifesto. Pasternak was not, of course, a genuine Futurist, but merely a Symbolist who had been influenced by a new formal language.

In the summer of 1914, Pasternak worked as a tutor for the family of the Lithuanian-Russian poet Jurgis Baltrušaitis in Petrovskoye on the Oka River. In July he met another guest, the other major theorist of Symbolism—Vyacheslav Ivanov. Over several weeks they conversed daily about the antagonisms within the new art. One of Ivanov's topics concerned occult clairvoyance,

Boris Pasternak, 1916.

a subject for which Pasternak had little sympathy.

While visiting his parents in Molodi in September, Pasternak read Emilii Medtner's recently published *Reflections on Goethe*. The work had a strong polemical edge, for it was intended to rescue Andrey Bely from occultism and attacked the entire Anthroposophical idea.

According to Medtner, Steiner's faculty of reason is incapable of dealing with symbols, and he is therefore unable to get any real grasp of Goethe. Our symbolic act of knowing would be inconceivable if, in accordance with Steiner's monistic model, we were able to establish and decipher everything. Goethe did not deny the objective existence of other dimensions of life, but merely took exception to arbitrary and systematic encroachments upon them. As he once declared, it is not given to us to grasp the truth, which is identical with the divine, directly—we perceive it only in reflection, in example and symbol.

After his trip to Italy, Medtner goes on, Goethe was in a war of love with nature. He felt he was nature's "fiancé" the moment he ceased being afraid and quit trying to violate it with theory, that is, as soon as he felt separate from it rather than vaguely fused with it. It was an act of necessity and therefore also of the highest freedom. His "marriage" with nature was perhaps the most harmonious union of private and public, personal and universal, in human history. He became godlike by heeding the exhortation of the Apollonian sun god: "Know thyself!" and penetrating deep within himself to the very core of his being. For Goethe, knowledge of the world was identical to knowledge of self.

Pasternak was utterly carried away by these comments. In the early fall of 1914, he sent Medtner a spontaneous letter in which he expressed his enthusiasm over the author's "youthful ardor and devilish sangfroid." Medtner's epistemological distinctions obviously must have appealed to him, as did his at once passionate and matter-of-fact scrutiny of Anthroposophy's monism. Here were Pasternak's own objections to Steiner in black and white. Surely even more important, however, was the fact that Medtner's portrayal of Goethe coincided with Pasternak's own view of art as expressed in "Symbolism and Immortality": at his most subjective, the artist becomes suprapersonal and touches upon experiences common to an entire generation.

To Medtner, who at the moment was on the brink of a breakdown, cut off from his native land, and watching the transformation of his cherished cultural synthesis into a horrific war between Germany and Russia, the letter meant a great deal. He found it not only lofty and sentimental, but also articulated with "talent and insight."

Medtner's difficult situation had prompted him to begin daily therapy with Jung. What was remarkable was that Jung and Pasternak seemed to be chiming in with each other. Sensing a kinship between Russian Symbolism and his own studies of symbols and myth, Jung was inclined to view Medtner as a kind of prophet. In his writings on Goethe, Medtner seemed to be moving toward Jung's own notion of the individual as the bearer of a hidden supraindividual experience.

Thus from different points of departure, Pasternak and Jung appear to have been attracted to the same thing in Medtner. Pasternak was looking for support of his idea about the immortal dimension of art, while Jung sought confirmation of his notion of a collective unconscious that speaks through art and myth. Both of them at this particular juncture in the fall of 1914 were in need of Medtner's ideas. In Jung's case all this eventually took shape in a psychological theory that was distinct from Freud's. As for Pasternak, the notion of immortality rooted in the Symbolist worldview became embodied in one of his crowning achievements, *Doctor Zhivago*. Written at the end of his life, at the same time when he was translating *Faust*, the novel was originally subtitled "Attempt at a Russian Faust."

MARIETTA SHAGINYAN
AND VERNER VON HEIDENSTAM

*M*arietta Shaginyan and Verner von Heidenstam... what could they possibly have in common — she a chronicler of the first Five Year Plan and a Soviet propagandist, he a Swedish aristocrat and aesthete? Yet at one historic moment in the wake of the October revolution, their paths unexpectedly converged. On February 25, 1918, the Baku newspaper *Kavkazskoe slovo* (*The Caucasian Word*) carried Shaginyan's enthusiastic review of the recently published Russian translation of Heidenstam's first novel, *Endymion* (1889). At this particular point in history, the work resonated with Shaginyan. Why was that? Let us take a look at how she came to write the review.

Shaginyan had been molded by the Russian Symbolist movement, in which life and art were an almost inseparable unity. At various times she had been a kind of "muse" to leading Symbolists and other modernist figures ranging from Andrey Bely to Sergey Rakhmaninov. Her life took a crucial turn in 1912, when she began an intense emotional and intellectual relationship with Emilii Medtner. For his part, he had a special need of her as his own personal crisis deepened.

Almost hypnotically, as Shaginyan herself put it, Medtner attempted over the course of several years to "enslave" her to his inexorable intellect. His aspiration was to use his Musagetes publishing house to push the entire Russian Symbolist movement westward. He was contemptuous of native Russian culture and objected in particular to what he considered to be Oriental features in it. Shaginyan came from a Christian Armenian family, and that background made her especially attractive to Medtner, who constantly sought the company of "Eastern" women. Now she energetically asserted an Eastern cultural identity in a desperate attempt to defend herself against his massive indoctrination. In 1913, she published the poetry collection *Orientalia*, which was dedicated to Sergey Rakhmaninov but essentially addressed to Medtner and his ideological tyranny. At the same time, well aware that Medtner regarded the Jewish "race" as destructively Oriental, she strongly condemned the anti-Semitic agitation behind the state-sponsored Beilis trial.

Shaginyan's essays around the time of Medtner's crisis contain an interesting discussion drawing on Goethe and others about human power plays and dominance aspirations. The articles demonstrate that she had by no means capitulated to his intellectual power. Beneath his need for control was a painful sense of inadequacy that he did not attempt to conceal and she knew how to manipulate. In sexually charged images in their correspondence, he occasionally described her as a brazen Amazon setting off in a wild gallop mounted on the tired old mare of his soul.

As Medtner began his therapy with Jung in the fall of 1914, Shaginyan was at first there with him in Zurich, but he found her a burden. She gradually broke free of his tight grip on her personality. The process began already there in Zurich when she happened to attend a meeting of émigré Bolsheviks just before she returned to Russia in November 1914. In this group she discovered a readiness for practical political action that fundamentally distinguished them from the morbidly self-centered Symbolists and their endless metaphysical ruminations. Soon, she began working on a novel that represented a settling of accounts with Medtner, Rakhmaninov, and the entire Symbolist outlook. Entitled *One's Own Fate*, it is set in a psychiatric clinic where a doctor treats impractical (recognizably Symbolist) neurotics by prohibiting them from discussing abstract subjects. At about the same time she wrote a positive review of a story by Pyotr Uspensky that had been influenced by the explicitly "practical" metaphysics of George Gurdjieff (who, like her, was of Armenian extraction).

In early 1917, Medtner finished his analysis with Jung in Zurich and began a new life. As for Shaginyan, she was prepared for *her*

Marietta Shaginyan, 1911.

new life. The Bolshevik seizure of power in the fall made a deep impression on her. She gradually became a Socialist, without on that account relinquishing her fundamentally religious outlook. The total transformation of life that Symbolism had seemed to offer soon acquired socialist overtones. From the very beginning she appears to be attracted to Bolshevism as an "Eastern" phenomenon. Vladimir Lenin became her new hero. It was she who would much later become the author of *The Ulyanov Family,* a major historical novel describing his personal background and political career. When Stalin came to power she felt even more at home in the new society: with a Caucasian like herself (who had moreover undoubtedly read her works) as the leader of Bolshevism, her own experience of the Revolution was confirmed once and for all.

At the turn of the year 1917-1918, when the fate of Russia hung in the balance after the October upheaval and she was moving toward Bolshevism, the 1916 Nobel Laureate Verner von Heidenstam appeared in Shaginyan's life with a novel that had an utterly liberating effect on her. It was serialized in the journal *Sovremenny mir* (*The Modern World*) during the summer of 1917 and the winter of 1918, with an interruption in the fall.

What was it about Heidenstam that appealed so strongly to Shaginyan at a time when the pain of separation from Symbolism was easing and she opened up to a new world view in which the catchwords were concreteness and practicality?

Endymion had once served as a protest against the naturalism of the 1880s in Sweden. It was a manifesto of the '90s on the boundary between the two decades that argued for sensualism and free artistic imagination, an anti-naturalistic tribute to strange and colorful ways of life. It repudiates Western civilization, which the young author proclaims is anemic and exhausted.

Endymion takes place on two skillfully interwoven levels. On the one hand it is the story about how the American Nelly Harven's views of reality are upset by her encounter with the Arab poet Emin and his Oriental outlook. On another level it is the history of a revolt led by Emin against colonial supremacy and a Western civilization that has been suffocating Muslims for centuries. Emin's revolt is crushed, but he has penetrated Nelly's hard shell: she returns home a different woman who acknowledges the spiritual superiority of Eastern ways of life.

The Western traveler visiting the Orient—Flaubert's *Voyage en Orient* being a typical example—was a recurrent theme in nineteenth-century literature. As Edward Said has shown, usually the "feminine" Orient was viewed through prejudiced masculine eyes as a harem fantasy or a brutal, cunningly evasive, underdeveloped civilization. The novelty in Heidenstam's work is that he reverses the concepts. Here it is a female traveler who observes and falls in love with a Muslim man, and the Orient is portrayed as superior in all respects. The Western "race," as he says, is spiritually hollow, despondent, rendered passive and unfit for life by its cult of suffering. The Arab "race" enjoys a far more harmonious, free, and joyful experience of existence.

It is not for nothing that Emin is a poet. Nelly herself dreams of becoming a writer. Traveling with her are her father, who writes humorous trifles, and a quack German doctor who bombards her with vacuous speechifying and, although he is protective of her, at bottom merely represents the hubris and shallowness of civilization.

There is an inner dialectic at work in both East and West, and everything is actually much more complicated than it seems. Emin is quite manly but also has clearly feminine features. The way the often rather masculine Nelly, guided by Emin, penetrates dark alleys and passageways bears a striking resemblance to the conventional pattern in depictions of the Orient, where the male Westerner is shown penetrating a female Eastern culture. The East is said to be living in an intense present unregulated by any clock, yet it is familiar with the delights of the past as well. At once both old and new, it embraces all eras. It is marked by ruin, yet it rises to revolt. The doom confronting the West is different. Although it continues to consolidate its dominion over the East, Western civilization is slowly decaying from within. Emin's rebellion is crushed, but, as Shaginyan maintains in her review, he preserves his dignity and is victorious on a deeper level. He meets his death, but his culture proves far more representative of life than does that of the West.

Shaginyan goes on to note that power is, of course, central to Emin and Nelly's relationship. Nelly feels she is culturally superior and repeatedly tries to put him in his place. He manages, however, to break her pride and shake her to the core. More than just a dreamy poet, he is prepared to defend his philosophy and ideals with deeds. Defying rationality, he aspires to guide history into new channels. His revolutionary action is consistent with his entire mysterious affirmation of life. Whereas the charlatan German doctor loses himself in empty verbiage and gestures, Emin unites poetry and bold action.

It is almost as though Heidenstam's novel was written especially for Shaginyan—not least its final chapter, which met her urgent needs at that particular moment. The work mirrored remarkably well the complexity of her dramatic relationship with Medtner, in which she, one suspects, empathized with the vibrant and sensual Oriental Emin and Medtner was cast in Nelly's feminine role as a representative of self-absorbed, self-congratulatory Western civilization. Shaginyan and Medtner's relations were similarly characterized by power and, eventually, reversed power positions. Shaginyan was at that very time about to come out in support of Lenin's "Eastern" revolution, the upheaval that Aleksandr Blok would portray in his 1918 poem as Russia's anti-Western "Scythian" face.

Shaginyan emphasizes in her review that Heidenstam depicts Islam as an earthly religion that has no need of supernatural holiness. It is a form of vitalism or worship of life that has sanctified all that is concrete and physically material. What the novel presents is not one faith against another, she maintains, but the rebellion of the

Muslim faith against Western unbelief, which has reduced religion to routine. "Socialism" can in fact be substituted for "Islam".

Marietta Shaginyan's life and works may appear to have gone through several different and diametrically opposed phases. At a deeper level, however, such is not the case. Her shift from Symbolism to socialism was skin-deep. In conversations with me in Peredelkino in December 1977 and Moscow in March 1981 (three months before her death at the age of 94), she stressed that Russia represents the East, that the West can never understand the East, and that Bolshevism had been guided all along by a higher religious purpose. Her transition from Symbolism to (ultimately) Stalinism provides more than a hint as to the kinship between the various early twentieth-century doctrines of liberation. There are unmistakable threads running between the utopian excesses and failures of the Symbolist dreamers and the immanent calamity of Russian "Real Socialism."

Literature[1]

Andrey Bely: Spirit of Symbolism. Edited by John E. Malmstad. Ithaca-London: Cornell University Press, 1987.
Asatiani, Michail. "Sluchai isterii s somnambulizmom i polovoi inverziei." *Psikhoterapiia* 2 (1914): 55-69.
Azadovskii, Konstantin, and Vladimir Kupchenko. "U istokov russkogo shteinerianstva." *Zvezda* 6 (1998): 146-191.
Belyi, Andrei. *Geheime Aufzeichnungen. Erinnerungen an das Leben im Umkreis Rudolf Steiners.* Translated by C. Hellmundt. Dornach: Rudolf Geering Verlag, 1992.
------. *Im Zeichen der Morgenröte. Erinnerungen an Aleksandr Blok.* Translated by Swetlana Geier. Basel: Zbinden Verlag, 1974.
------. *Mezhdu dvukh revoliutsii.* Edited by Aleksandr Lavrov. Moscow: Khudozhestvennaia literatura, 1990.
------. *Nachalo veka.* Edited by Aleksandr Lavrov. Moscow: Khudozhestvennaia literatura, 1990.
------. *Na rubezhe dvukh stoletii.* Edited by Aleksandr Lavrov. Moscow: Khudozhestvennaia literatura, 1989.
------. *O Bloke.* Edited by Aleksandr Lavrov. Moscow: Avtograf, 1997.
------. *Peterburg.* Edited by Leonid Dolgopolov. Moscow: Nauka, 1981.
------. *Rudol'f Shteiner i Gete v mirovozzrenii sovremennosti. Vospominaniia o Shteinere.* Edited by Irina Lagutina and Monika Spivak. Moscow: Respublika, 2000.
------. *Serebrianyi golub'.* Edited by Michail Koz'menko. Moscow: Khudozhestvennaia literatura, 1989.
------. *Simfonii.* Edited by Aleksandr Lavrov. Leningrad: Khudozhestvennaia literatura, 1991.
------. *Simvolizm kak miroponimanie.* Edited by Larisa Sugai. Moscow: Respublika, 1994.

---

[1] The references to Russian editions are given in accordance with the Library of Congress transliteration system; the spellings of some names may vary from the spellings used in the text and in references to editions in languages other than Russian.

Literature

------. *Stichotvoreniia i poemy*, t. 1-2. Edited by Aleksandr Lavrov and Dzhon Malmstad. St. Petersburg-Moscow: Akademicheskii proekt/ Progress-Pleiada, 2006.
------. *Tragediia tvorchestva*. Moscow: Musaget, 1911.
------. "*Vash rytsar'*". *Pis'ma k M. K. Morozovoi 1901-1928*. Edited by Aleksandr Lavrov and Dzhon Malmstad. Moscow: Progress-Pleiada, 2006.
------. *Verwandeln des Lebens. Erinnerungen an Rudolf Steiner*. Translated by Swetlana Geier. Basel: Futurum Verlag, 2011.
Belyi, Andrei, and Aleksandr Blok. *Perepiska 1903-1919*. Edited by Aleksandr Lavrov. Moscow: Progress-Pleiada, 2001.
Berdiaev, Nikolai. *Samopoznanie (Opyt filosofskoi avtobiografii)*. Moscow: Mezhdunarodnye otnosheniia, 1990.
Blok, Aleksandr. "Perepiska s Vl. Piastom." Edited by Zara Mints. In *Literaturnoe nasledstvo. Aleksandr Blok. Novye materialy i issledovaniia*, t. 92:2. Moscow: Nauka, 1981.
------. *Polnoe sobranie sochinenii i pisem v dvadtsati tomakh*, t. 1-5, 7-8. Edited by Natal'ia Griakalova et al. Moscow: Nauka, 1997-2010.
Bogomolov, Nikolai. *Russkaia literatura nachala XX veka i okkul'tizm*. Moscow: Novoe Literaturnoe Obozrenie, 1999.
Carlson, Maria. "*No Religion Higher than Truth.*" *A History of the Theosophical Movement in Russia, 1875-1922*. Princeton, NJ: Princeton University Press, 1993.
Ellis. *Neizdannoe i nesobrannoe*. Tomsk: Vodolei, 2000.
------. *Stikhotvoreniia*. Tomsk: Vodolei, 1996.
"Epistoliarnye materialy. M.A. Polivanova - F.M. Dostoevskomu." Edited by Ol'ga Ipatova. In *Dostoevskii. Materialy i issledovaniia*, t. 13: 263-276. St. Petersburg: Nauka, 1996.
Etkind, Aleksandr. *Eros nevozmozhnogo. Istoriia psikhoanaliza v Rossii*. St. Petersburg: Meduza, 1993.
Fedjuschin, Viktor B. *Russlands Sehnsucht nach Spiritualität. Theosophie, Anthroposophie und die Russen*. Schaffhausen: Novalis Verlag, 1988.
Gertsyk, Evgeniia. *Liki i obrazy*. Moscow: Molodaia gvardiia, 2007.
Giatsintova, Sof'ia. *S pamiat'iu naedine*. Moscow: Iskusstvo, 1989.
Il'in, Ivan. *Sobranie sochinenii*, t. 1-29. Edited by Iurii Lisitsa. Moscow: Russkaia kniga, 1993-2013.
Ivanov, Viacheslav. *Sobranie sochinenii*, t. I-IV. Brussels: Foyer Oriental Chrétien, 1971-87.
Janko Lavrin i Rossiia. Edited by Iuliia Sozina. Moscow: Rossiiskaia Akademiia Nauk/Institut Slavianovedeniia, 2011.
Jung, Carl Gustav. *Erinnerungen, Träume, Gedanken*. Edited by Aniela Jaffé. Zurich-Dusseldorf: Walter-Verlag, 1984.
Knigoizdatel'stvo "Musaget": Istoriia. Mify. Rezul'taty. Materialy i issledovaniia. Edited by Anna Reznichenko. Moscow, 2014.

Kobilinski-Ellis, Leo. *Alexander Puschkin. Der religiöse Genius Russlands.* Olten: Otto Walter Verlag, 1948.
------. "Die Macht des Weinens und des Lachens. Zur Seelengeschichte Nikolaus Gogols." In N. Gogol: *Betrachtungen über die göttliche Liturgie:* 80-100. Freiburg: Herder-Verlag, 1938.
------. *W. A. Joukowski. Seine Persönlichkeit, sein Leben und sein Werk.* Paderborn: Schöningh, 1933.
Lavrov, Aleksandr. *Andrei Belyi. Razyskaniia i etiudy.* Moscow: Novoe Literaturnoe Obozrenie, 2007.
------. *Andrei Belyi v 1900-e gody. Zhizn' i literaturnaia deiatel'nost'.* Moscow: Novoe Literaturnoe Obozrenie, 1995.
------. *Russkie simvolisty. Etiudy i razyskaniia.* Moscow: Progress-Pleiada, 2007.
Ljunggren, Magnus. *The Russian Mephisto. A Study of the Life and Work of Emilii Medtner.* Stockholm: Almqvist & Wiksell International, 1994.
------. *Twelve Essays on Andrej Belyj's Peterburg.* Gothenburg: Acta Universitatis Gothoburgensis, 2009.
Malmstad, Dzhon. "Andrei Belyi i antroposofiia." In *Minuvshee* t. 6: 337-448. Paris: Atheneum, 1988.
------. "Andrei Belyi i antroposofiia." In *Minuvshee* t. 8: 409-472. Paris: Atheneum, 1989.
------. "Andrei Belyi i antroposofiia." In *Minuvshee* t. 9: 409-488. Paris: Atheneum, 1990.
Maydell, Renata von. *Vor dem Thore. Ein Vierteljahrhundert Anthroposophie in Russland.* Munich: Projekt Verlag, 2005.
Medtner, Emil. "Bildnis der Persönlichkeit im Rahmen des gegenseitigen Sich Kennenlernens." In *Die kulturelle Bedeutung der komplexen Psychologie.* Edited by Linda Fierz, Emil Medtner, and Toni Wolff: 556-616. Berlin: Verlag von Julius Springer, 1935.
------. "Jungs 'Psychologische Typen'." *Neue Zürcher Zeitung,* 16/17 June 1921.
------. Letters to Anna and Nikolai Medtner. Library of Congress, Washington, Musical Library, 31:43 (The Rakhmaninov Archive).
------. *Über die sog. Intuition, die ihr angrenzenden Begriffe und die an sie anknüpfenden Probleme.* Moscow-Zurich: Verlag Musagetes, 1923.
Metner, Emilii. *Modernizm i muzyka.* Moscow: Musaget, 1912.
------. Pis'ma Anne Mikhailovne Metner. RO RGB (Rossiiskaia Gosudarstvennaia Biblioteka/Russian State Library), Moscow, f. 167.
------. *Razmyshleniia o Gete. Razbor vzgliadov R. Shteinera v sviazi s voprosami krititsizma, simvolizma i okkul'tizma.* Moscow: Musaget, 1914.
Mochulskii, Konstantin. *Vladimir Solov'ev. Zhizn' i uchenie.* Moscow: Direktmedia Pablishing, 2008.

"N. A. Berdiaev ob antroposofii. Dva pis'ma Andreiu Belomu." *Novyi zhurnal* 137 (1979): 118-123.
Nefed'ev, Georgii. "'Moia dusha raskrylas' dlia vsego chudesnogo...' Prilozhenie: Perepiska S. N. Durylina i Ellisa (1909-1910 gg.)." In *S. N. Durylin i ego vremia. Kniga pervaia. Issledovaniia*, edited by Anna Reznichenko: 113-158. Moscow, 2010.
Obatnin, Gennadii. *Ivanov-mistik: okkul'tnye motivy v poezii i proze Viacheslava Ivanova (1907-1919)*. Moscow: Novoe Literaturnoe Obozrenie, 2000.
Pamiati L. I. Polivanova (K 10-letiiu so dnia smerti). Moscow: Obshchestvo byvshikh vospitannikov gimnazii L. I. Polivanova, 1909.
Pasternak, Boris. *Okhrannaia gramota*. Moscow: Kniga po Vostrebovaniiu, 2011.
Piast, Vladimir. *Vstrechi*. Edited by Roman Timenchik. Moscow: Novoe Literaturnoe Obozrenie, 1997.
------. "Avgust Strindberg (Vmesto nekrologa)." *Novaia zhizn'* 5 (1912): 203-212.
Pisateli simvolistskogo kruga. Novye materialy. Edited by V. Bystrov, Natal'ia Griakalova, and Aleksandr Lavrov. St. Petersburg: Dmitrii Bulanin, 2000.
Polivanova, Mariia. "Zapis' o poseshchenii Dostoevskogo 9 iiunia 1880." In *F. M. Dostoevskii v vospominaniiakh sovremennikov*, t. 2: 357-364. Moscow: Khudozhestvennaia literatura, 1990.
Poljakov, Fedor. *Literarische Profile von Lev Kobylinskij-Ėllis im Tessiner Exil. Forschungen - Texte - Kommentare*. Köln-Weimar-Wien: Böhlau Verlag, 2000.
Pyman, Avril. *The Life of Aleksandr Blok*, in 2 vols. Oxford: Oxford University Press, 1979-80.
Rice, James L. *Freud's Russia. National Identity in the Evolution of Psychoanalysis*. New Brunswick-London: Transaction Publishers, 1993.
Shaginian, Marietta. *Svoia sud'ba*. Leningrad: Izdatel'stvo pisatelei, 1928.
------. "Vostok cherez shveda (O romane G. Geierstama (*sic*; M.L.) 'Endimion')." *Kavkazskoe slovo*, 25 February 1918.
Smirnoff, Karin. "Minnen." Kungliga Bibliotekets handskriftsarkiv (The Royal Swedish Library Manuscript Archive), Stockholm, dep. 233, XXI.
Smirnoff, Vladimir. "August Strindbergs sista dagar." *Afton-Tidningen*, 14 May 1942: 5.
------. "Minnen av en härlig rebell." *Vi*, 9 May 1942: 3, 14.
Solov'ev, Sergei. "Aleksei Venkstern." *Vesy* 6 (1909): 89-92.
------. *Sobranie stikhotvorenii*. Edited by V. Skripkina/Stefano Garzonio. Moscow: Vodolei, 2007.
------. *Vospominaniia*. Edited by Svetlana Misochnik/V. Nekhotin. Moscow: Novoe Literaturnoe Obozrenie, 2003.

------. *Zhizn' i tvorcheskaia evoliutsiia Vladimira Solov'eva*. Edited by Igor' Vishnevetskii. Moscow: Respublika, 1997.
Solov'ev, Vladimir. *Sobranie sochinenii v desiati tomakh*. St. Petersburg: Prosveshchenie, 1911-14.
------. *Sochineniia v dvukh tomakh*. Edited by Nikolai Kotrelev/Evgenii Rashkovskii. Moscow: Pravda, 1988-89.
Spivak, Monika. *Andrei Belyi – mistik i sovetskii pisatel'*. Moscow: Rossiiskii Gosudarstvennyi Gumanitarnyi Universitet, 2006.
Sventsitskii, Valentin. *Antikhrist (Zapiski strannogo cheloveka)*. St. Petersburg: Knizhnyi magazin "Luch" S. Tsukermana, 1908.
------. *Intelligentsiia*. Moscow: Portugalov, 1912.
------. *Smert'. Drama v trekh deistviiakh. Pastor Relling. Drama v trekh deistviiakh*. Moscow: Knizhnyi magazin "Trud", 1909.
Tsvetaeva, Marina. "Charodei." In *Sobranie sochinenii v semi tomakh*, v. 3. Edited by Anna Saakiants and Lev Mnukhin: 6-15. Moscow: Ellis Lak, 1994.
Vishniak, Mark. *Dan' proshlomu*. New York: Izdatel'stvo imeni Chekhova, 1954.
Voloshin, Maksimilian. *Stikhotvoreniia i poemy*. St. Petersburg: Nauka, 1995.
Vzyskuiushchie Grada. Khronika chastnoi zhizni russkikh religioznykh filosofov v pis'makh i dnevnikakh. Edited by Vladimir Keidan. Moscow: Iazyki russkoi kul'tury, 1997.
Willich, Heide. *Lev L. Kobylinskij-Ėllis. Vom Symbolismus zur ars sacra*. Munich: Verlag Otto Sagner, 1996.
The Wolf-Man by the Wolf-Man. Edited by Muriel Gardiner. New York: Basic Books, 1976.
Woloschin, Margarita. *Die grüne Schlange. Lebenserinnerungen*. Stuttgart: Deutsche Verlags-Anstalt, 1968.

Index of Names

Adler, A.   90–92
Adler, R.   92
Alexander II   116
Anisimov, Yu.   135
Artsybashev, M.   38
Asatiani, M.   65, 95
Aseev, N.   135
Azef, E.   35, 38–40, 42
Ball, H.   27, 28
Balmont, K.   45
Baltrušaitis, J.   135
Baudelaire, C.   134
Beilis, M.   48, 139
Bekhterev, V.   95
Belinsky, V.   44
Bely, A.   8–26, 28, 30, 31, 36, 37, 40–43, 45, 47–53, 58, 66, 70, 72, 97–103, 105–110, 112–114, 117–119, 121, 122, 124, 125, 127, 128, 130–134, 136, 138
Berdyaev, N.   31, 37, 99–102, 104, 105
Bergh, R.   81, 85
Bernstein, A.   89
Besant, A.   45
Blavatsky, H.   (Blavatskaya, E.) 44, 45
Blok, A.   11–13, 15, 18–25, 43, 50, 68–74, 76–87, 99, 101–103, 122, 142
Blok, L.   (Mendeleeva, L.) 12, 19–22, 24, 70, 71, 79, 80, 82–86
Bobrov, S.   135
Bondi, Yu.   82
Botticelli, S.   129
Brikhnichyov, I.   40, 42
Bryusov, V.   45
Bugaev, B., see Bely, A.
Bugaev, N.   12, 108
Bulgakov, M.   66, 67
Bulgakov, S.   37–40, 99, 101–103

Bunin, I.   95
Burtsev, V.   38
Chaadaev, P.   62
Chagall, M.   57
Chamberlain, H. S.   125
Charcot, J. M.   93
Charles XII   61
Chekhov, A.   66
Chekhov, M.   66
Ciganović, M.   59
Cohen, H.   134
Dante Alighieri   130
Darwin, C.   8
Dickens, C.   66
Dobrolyubov, A.   27, 28
Dostoevsky, F.   18, 23, 24, 28, 29, 34, 35, 37, 50, 54, 56, 60, 92, 96, 98, 112, 115, 118
Droznes, L.   93, 96
Dubois, P.   89
Eitingon, M.   91, 93
Ellis, see Kobylinsky, L.
Ern, V.   35, 37, 40
Essad Pasha   59
Feinberg, E.   17
Feltsman, O.   88, 89, 95
Ferenczi, S.   90
Flaubert, G.   69
Francia, F.   129
Freud, S.   13, 64, 66, 88–94, 96, 97, 115–119, 122, 125–128, 137
Gapon, G.   41
Gertsyk, E.   43, 46
Giatsintov, V.   63
Giatsintova, S.   13, 63, 64, 65, 66, 67
Ginzburg, V.   17
Gippius, Z.   35
Glière, R.   135
Goebbels, J.   123

149

Index of Names

Goethe, J. W.   78, 102, 106, 117, 122, 124–126, 128–132, 134–137
Gogol, N.   18, 21, 23, 31, 33, 41, 51, 76, 92
Goncharova, N.   57
Gorodetsky, S.   46, 56, 58
Gurdjieff, G.   60
Gurevich, L.   116, 121
Gurevich, Ya.   116
Hahn, E.   (Gan, E.) 44
Hamnqvist, H.   77
Hegel, F.   117
Heidenstam, V.   von 138, 140, 142
Herzen, A.   37
Hitler, A.   122, 132
Hugo, V.   31
Husserl, E.   116
Ibsen, H.   35, 37, 40, 45, 66, 72, 73
Ilyin, A.   116
Ilyin, I. I   116
Ilyin, I. II   97, 106, 115–123, 125, 129
Ilyina, N.   119
Ivanov, V.   31, 43, 46–50, 99–101, 113, 119–121, 135
Jung, C. G.   65, 88, 97, 106, 123, 128–133, 137
Jung, E.   133
Junker, V.   80
Kachalov, V.   64, 65
Kannabikh, Yu.   13, 89, 90, 97
Kant, I.   106, 124–126
Kaus, O.   92
Khlebnikov, V.   57, 58, 59
Kobilinski-Ellis, L., see Kobylinsky, L.
Kobylinskaya, V.   28, 29
Kobylinsky, I.   28, 29
Kobylinsky, L. (Ellis, Kobilinski-Ellis, L.)   26–34, 48, 98, 102–104, 106
Kobylinsky, S.   29
Kovalenskaya, A.   10
Krakht, K.   134
Kruchonykh, A.   59
Kulbin, N.   80–82, 84, 86
Kuprin, A.   95
Kusevitsky, S.   120, 121
Kustodiev, B.   55
Kuzmin, M.   46, 49
Larionov, M.   57
Lavrin, J. (I.)   54–60
Le Dantue, M.   56, 57, 59
Lenin, V. (Ulyanov, V.)   66, 115, 140, 142

Lermontov, M.   62, 96
Leshkova, O.   59
Lippi, F.   129
Malevich, K.   57
Marx, K.   8, 105
Masaryk, T.   54, 55, 57, 60
Mayakovsky, V.   57
Medtner, A.   125, 127
Medtner, E.   23, 47, 48, 51, 86, 97, 101–104, 106, 109, 116, 117, 119, 122–133, 136–139, 142
Medtner, N.   116, 117, 119–121, 124, 125, 127
Mendeleev, D.   70, 71
Mendeleeva, A.   71
Mendeleeva, L., see Blok, L.
Merezhkovsky, D.   35, 41, 96, 97, 102, 103
Meulen, J. van der   30–31
Meyerhold, V.   80, 82, 83
Mgebrov, A.   80, 82
Mintslov, R. Jr.   44
Mintslov, R. Sr.   43
Mintslov, S.   44
Mintslova, A.   43–53
Moreto y Cabaña, A.   63
Mussolini, B.   122, 132
Nesterov, M.   123
Nietzsche, F.   8, 11, 18, 45, 99, 113, 114, 129
Nikola, King   59
Novalis (Hardenberg, F. von)   45, 135
Orage, A. R.   60
Orlenev, P.   40
Osipov, N.   89–91, 95
Pankeev, K.   93–95, 97
Pankeev, S.   92–97, 118
Pasternak, B.   134–137
Pasternak, L.   31
Peter I (the Great)   61, 97, 112
Pirosmani, N.   57
Plehve, V.   94
Pobedonostsev, K.   36
Polivanov, L. (Zagarin, L.)   28, 29, 33, 34, 63
Polivanova, M.   28, 29
Princip, G.   59
Pronin, B.   80
Pushkin, A.   18, 19, 23, 28, 29, 32–34, 42, 62, 112
Pyast, V.   (Pestovsky, V.) 68, 69, 71, 73, 74, 76–78, 80, 82, 84–87

150

Index of Names

Rakhmaninov, S.   120, 123, 138, 139
Rasputin, G.   42
Remizov, A.   82, 102
Rice, J.   93
Rilke, R. M.   135
Rosenberg, A.   123
Rot, V.   63, 64
Rozanov, V.   39
Ryf, M.   110
Sabashnikova, M.   46
Said, E.   141
Sapunov, N.   80, 82
Savinkov, B.   38
Schiller, F.   126
Scriabin, A.   117, 120, 121, 134
Serbsky, V.   95
Shaginyan, M.   125, 138, 139, 140, 142
Shakespeare, W.   63, 69
Sikorsky, I.   12
Simmel, G.   116
Smirnoff, K.   (Strindberg, K.) 73, 75–77, 82–86
Smirnoff, W.   (V.) 73–76, 82–86
Solovyov, M.   10, 11
Solovyov, S.   10–21, 32, 62, 64, 65, 70, 97, 102, 103
Solovyov, V.   8, 10, 11, 14, 15, 18, 19, 27, 28, 32, 34, 35, 41, 45, 48, 98
Solovyova, O.   I 10
Solovyova, O.   II 16
Sophocles   86
Spielrein, S.   65, 88, 90
Stalin, J. (Dzhugashvili, I.)   40, 52, 115, 140
Stanislavsky, K.   64, 121
Steiner, R.   27, 31, 45, 47, 49, 51–53, 58, 98–110, 112, 114, 117, 122, 124–126, 130, 136, 137
Stekel, W.   90, 92
Stember, N.   127
Stepun, F.   134
Strindberg, A.   68–71, 73–82, 84–87, 99
Strindberg, G.   82
Strindberg, K. (see Smirnoff, K.)
Sventsitsky, V.   35–42
Taneev, S.   45
Taneev, V.   45
Teresa of Avila, St.   30
Tolstoy, L.   50, 54–56, 73, 91, 96
Trotsky, L.   91
Trüb, G.   133

Trüb, H.   133
Trubetskoy, E.   122
Tsvetaeva, M.   26
Turgenev, I.   24, 63
Turgeneva, A.   14, 24, 50, 51, 102, 108, 111, 130
Turgeneva, N.   (Pozzo, N.) 130
Turgeneva, T.   14
Ulyanov, V., see Lenin, V.
Ulyanova, M.   66
Uspensky, P.   139
Venkstern, A(leksandra)   62
Venkstern, A. Jr.   61–65, 94
Venkstern, A. Sr.   62
Venkstern, Kh.   61
Venkstern, N.   63–67
Venkstern, O.   62
Venkstern, Ya. I (Wenckstern, J.)   61
Venkstern, Ya. II   62
Verigina, V.   80, 82–84, 86
Virgil   130
Vishnyak, M.   35, 36, 41
Volkonskaya, M.   34
Volkonsky, N.   34
Voloshin, M.   43, 45, 46, 51, 104
Vrubel, A.   68
Vrubel, M.   68
Vulf, M.   (Woolf, M.) 90, 91, 93
Vyakhirev, A.   64–66
Vyrubov, N.   88–90, 92
Vyrubova, N.   90
Wagner, R.   134
Weininger, O.   116
Wenckstern, C.   61
Wenckstern, J., see Venkstern, Ya.
Wolff, T. (A.)   132
Zdanevich, I.   57, 59
Zdanevich, K.   57, 59
Zhukovsky, V.   32, 33
Zinovyeva-Annibal, L.   46
Zweig, S.   118

Andrey Bely's "Lifeline"

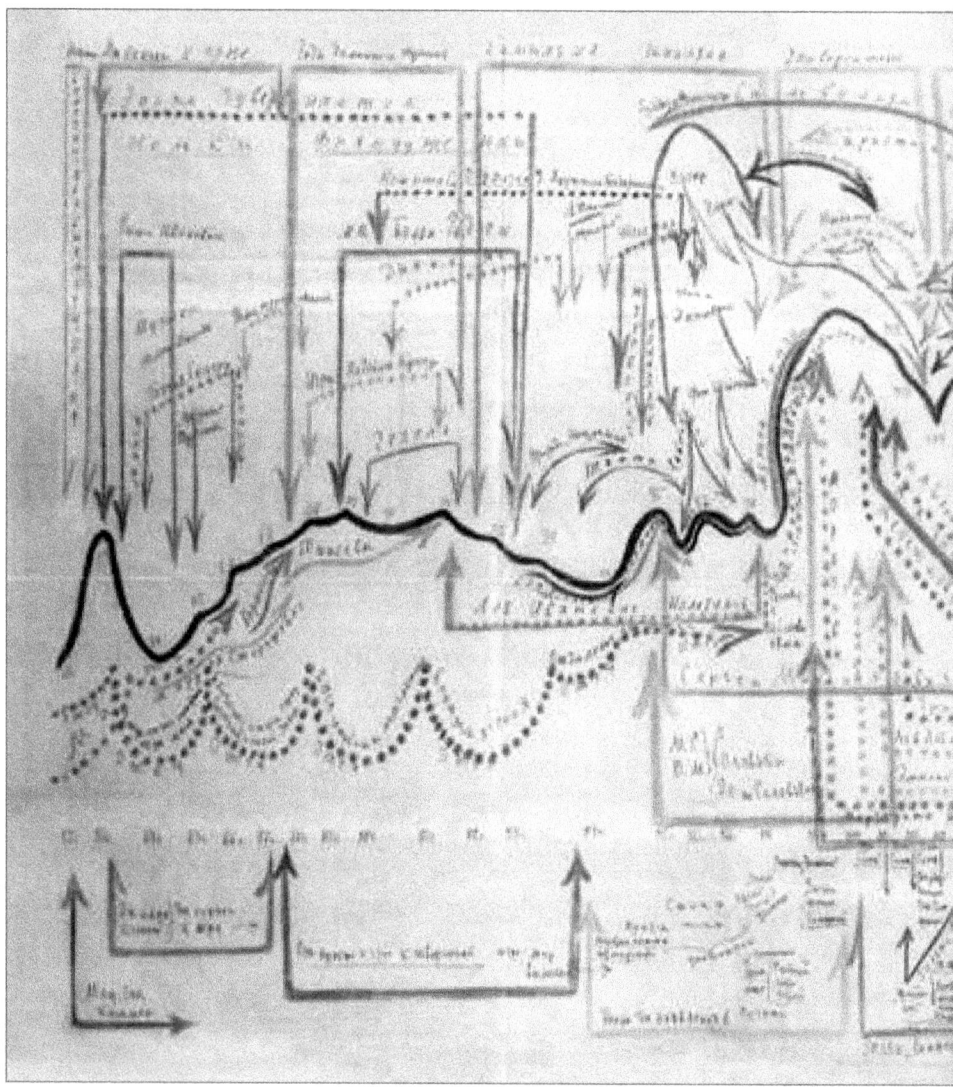

Bely's "Lifeline"—an attempt to summarize his personal and artistic evolution and important influences from his first conscious moments in 1883 at the age of 2-3 up to 1927, when he drew the sketch (illustration to the chapter "Bely's Encounter with Rudolf Steiner," pp. 107-114).

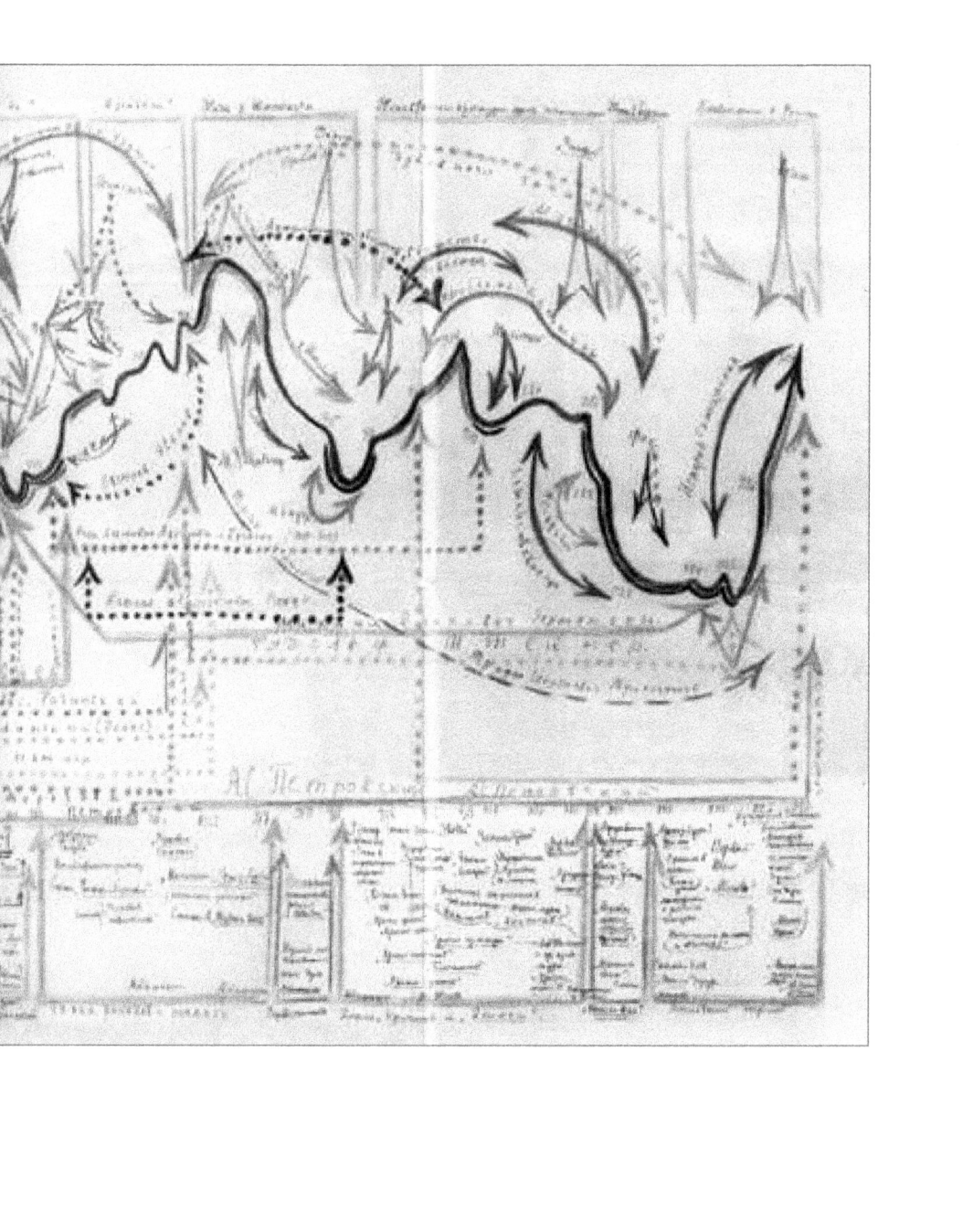